IT HAPPENED TOMORROW:

It'll Happen Again Yesterday,

A Brief History of Willful Amnesia -
When Memory of the Future Fails Us

W. E. Gutman

CCB Publishing
British Columbia, Canada

It Happened Tomorrow: It'll Happen Again Yesterday, A Brief
History of Willful Amnesia – When Memory of the Future Fails Us

Copyright ©2024 by W. E. Gutman
ISBN-13 978-1-77143-611-3
First Edition

Library and Archives Canada Cataloguing in Publication
Title: It happened tomorrow : it'll happen again yesterday, a brief history of willful amnesia –
when memory of the future fails us / W.E. Gutman.
Names: Gutman, W. E., 1937- author.
Description: First edition.
Issued in print and electronic formats.
Identifiers: ISBN 978-1-77143-611-3 (pbk.).--ISBN 978-1-77143-612-0 (pdf)
Additional cataloguing data available from Library and Archives Canada

Cover image: AI-generated image by the author using Public Domain images.

This book is printed on acid-free paper.

Extreme care has been taken by the author to ensure that all information presented in
this book is accurate and up to date at the time of publishing. The publisher cannot
be held responsible for any errors or omissions. Additionally, neither is any liability
assumed by the publisher for damages resulting from the use of the information
contained herein.

Publisher: CCB Publishing
              British Columbia, Canada
              www.ccbpublishing.com

"What has been will be,
and what was done will be done.
There is nothing new under the sun."
Attributed to King Solomon, Ecclesiastes 1:4-11

"If you want to know who controls you,
look at who you are not allowed to criticize."
Voltaire (1694-1778)

PROLOGUE
Life: The dream we're forced to remember

Trapped between two imponderables — an immovable past that elicits no remorse and an unfathomable tomorrow we steadfastly erode with every word we utter (or fail to utter), every action we take (or spinelessly abstain from taking) — we stagnate in a never-ending now for which we take no responsibility and which we are loath to change. We seek to be absolved of our own inequities by ignoring them. Yesterday is gone. Oh, well. Nothing deadens scruples like a clear conscience. Nothing threatens the present — and the future — like willful, preconceptual amnesia of an unchanging past. In more prosaic terms, past is prologue. By ignoring it, we are doomed to recreate it.

⁂

Surely, the double-take-producing title of this book is bizarre, arresting, even absurd. But it is not a syntactic incongruity, a deliberate affront to grammar, the trance-like, otherworldly divination of a mystic or the hallucinatory ramblings of a paranoiac. It's a child's surreal, apostrophic, anguished non sequitur exclaimed as he emerged from a dream whose terrifying images, fed by what he had overheard the night before, spoke of a reality that far exceeded anything he might heretofore have imagined. I was that child: My paternal grandparents and two of their sons, I had learned, and an untold number of fathers and mothers and sons and daughters, had perished in Auschwitz, the largest and arguably the most notorious of all the Nazi death camps.

Like all children, I had no concept of time. Immersed in a world in which fantasy competed with materiality, the rhythms of daily life were elusive abstractions forever interrupted by evanescent moments of conscious actuality. Yesterday, today, and tomorrow were mere words, adult words that had no intrinsic meaning. I was four.

A year earlier, I had been treated to a phantasmagoric spectacle: France's unchallenged invasion by the Germans. I can still hear in my mind's ears the rhythmic clatter of German boots stomping on the Champs Élysées. I was five when I witnessed my father's brutal arrest by the Gestapo and when, upon his miraculous escape, he, my mother, and I beat a hasty retreat from occupied Paris with the shirts on our backs. I was six when ten old men, eight among them veterans of the "Great War," were dragged to the village square, lined up against the church wall and shot to avenge the murder of a German officer who'd been screwing the butcher's daughter. I saw them crumple, limp, lifeless on the cobbled sidewalk. I remember staring at the pitiful assemblage of inert, scrunched cadavers, blood oozing from their open mouths, their lifeless eyes staring in the void like those of a doll. I also remember telling myself over and over that I'd been treated to a monstrous yet otherwise banal spectacle, a dramatization of unimaginable realism, yet mere cinema. It began to rain. The steady downpour rinsed away the blood as onlookers, crossing themselves, their heads bowed, scattered and vanished in a gray sulfur-laden mist. The butcher's daughter survived the war only to have her head shaved in a public orgy of bestiality and later beaten to death by exultant French freedom fighters, many of whom had screwed France to the bone when no one was looking. And I remember the mournful peal of church bells, loud enough to deafen those who heard it, but apparently inaudible to or shamelessly unnoticed by the all-seeing, all-hearing, all-knowing *god* in whom the faithful put their trust.

Teeming with foreboding and childhood memories mutilated by the passage of time, fleeting, impenetrable, maddening, my dreams would hereafter telegraph repressed emotions, they would disinter buried fears, and warn against senseless expectations. I still get lost in the fog of my nocturnal meanderings, in search of nonexistent locales or, worse, of familiar ones that keep receding the closer I get, or that break up and disperse like quicksilver. The dream I weaved that night hinted at a precocious gift of clairvoyance. What's to come, I ventured, borrows from what's already been. It was at that moment of numbing sorrow that I began to question the existence of *god* — to whom I had never been introduced and who failed to materialize no matter how hard I looked. Millions of my fellow Jews had gone up in smoke in Hitler's ovens and the inscrutability of *god*'s designs, at best an offensive rationale, had suddenly acquired a loathsome aftertaste.

I rejected predestination and the contemptible assertion that man is born sullied by some primal sin, that pain ennobles the soul, and that sentient beings need to be ruled by a system of coerced, arbitrary, faith-based dictums and protocols. In religion's ostensible virtues and objectives, I discovered not a path to enlightenment or serenity but an instrument of deceit and spiritual enslavement. I understood instinctively that man enacts laws (or enforces commandments) that are impossible to obey, thus justifying ruthless reprisals against the wayward. As Woody Allen memorably remarked,

> *"Some men will follow any order no matter how asinine as long as it comes from a resonant, well-modulated voice."*

The makeover from insouciant fence-straddler to outspoken mutineer was gradual, filled with misgivings. At first, I found religion's mystique inscrutable. I had meandered through its occluded allegories and bizarre canons and affectations like an explorer in a strange, uncharted wilderness. I had searched for the very faint light that faith purports to shed but found only vast and gloomy shadows. It is in the shadows that my senses, now accustomed to the darkness, caught sight of a glow, a radiant luminosity that rinsed my pupils free of the gritty debris of credulity. I understood that absurd beliefs, not glaring truths, prejudice, superstition, and groundless fear, not common sense, threaten humankind and commit it to eternal bondage. I had absent-mindedly glossed over sundry propositions and perspectives along the way, some of which I even peddled, parrot-like, out of ignorance, naïveté, or mental sloth.

Forty years later, still questioning, anxious to jettison some of my own dismissive preconceptions, eager to understand the universe and my place in it, I boldly ventured into the Kabbalah's arcane entrails. Enthralled and bewildered, often driven to mental exhaustion, I soon tired of its multilayered opaqueness, contradictions, and maddening esotericism. I was not being ushered into some liberating "beyond." Rather, I was being shoved and jostled and conned to probe nothingness and eternity, corporality and illusion, omnipresence, and non-existence. I found such mental pirouettes more taxing than I'd imagined. Faced with the imponderable—the very essence of mysticism—I quietly bowed out, humbled by the magic of paradox.

All things considered, my brief foray into the arcane corridors of god and the universe would not be in vain. Careful, measured readings yielded fresh insights on the richness of Jewish thought. I would later marvel at the influence it would have on the works of Pico Della Mirandola (1463-1494), Baruch Spinoza (1632-1677), Gottfried Leibniz (1646-1716), Emmanuel Swedenborg (1688-1772), Franz Kafka (1883-1924), Sigmund Freud (1856-1939), Walter Benjamin (1892-1940), Jorge Luis Borges (1899-1986), and Jacques Derrida (1930-2004). I must believe that I too was transformed, however imperceptibly, by the Kabbalah's wrenching cerebral exactions and staggering incomprehensibility. I then turned to the Tao, Buddhism, Sikhism, and the Quran. I probed the Tanya (the 18th century work of Hasidic mystical psychology) not to discover god but to fill the gaps in my monumental and increasing ignorance, to find answers where I had not yet looked. In search of irrefutable verities, I found myself struggling to reconcile conflicting arguments and put an end to self-created doubts. all in an effort to discover what ignorance prevents me from knowing. I've been re-reading—slowly, painfully, one sentence at a time—*The Guide for the Perplexed* by the great medieval Jewish philosopher, Maimonides (1138-1204), who held that there are significant limitations to what human beings can demonstrate empirically—an assertion that angered both Jews and Christians as it insinuated, they claimed, that *god*'s existence cannot be proven. It still can't. Now, do I really understand any more about life, the human psyche, and the multiverse—if one really exists? Should I rejoice because the cosmos might be made up of an endless series of timelines or bubbles ... that I am actually the product of someone else's dream ... or that I am a figment of my own imagination--as I argue in one of my dystopias?* I avoid asking why as I'd have to fall back on other people's limited knowledge and theories. Matter is the central substance in nature, and all things, including mental states result from material interactions, some of which we engineer, others that are imposed upon us.

Whatever trace of idealism I might have possessed has long since been replaced by cynicism and disgust at man's inability or unwillingness to advance outside his primal state. Theories, like doctrinal beliefs, have an academic appeal—it is interesting to plumb the limits of human imagination—but they do not hold for me the same allure as the observable, palpable universe around me. This could explain why I stopped reading novels more than thirty years ago. I find fact—in all disciplines—far more illuminating.

---

* *One Last Dream,* by W. E. Gutman, ©2012, CCB Publishing.

Eventually, I concluded that *god* is a useless and costly illusion with which I can easily dispense. Crypto-agnosticism blossomed into overt and liberating atheism as I finally awoke from the slumber of childhood innocence. Millions had perished in Hitler's gas chambers and the *inscrutability* of *god*'s designs, at best an offensive rationale, had suddenly acquired a loathsome aftertaste. So much for the dream.

⊗⊱

This book explores three converging themes, all predictive of the same end-result. The first, without which the other two cannot take place, deals with the relativistic nature of time—an interval we can neither consciously experience nor regulate. The second and third, least assumptive, remind us that, as a function of human folly, empires—like massive stars that explode luminously on their final journey to extinction—also reach their apogee then collapse. The larger the star, the more massive the conflagration. Nothing lasts forever. Extinction is part of the evolution of life. Both processes elude attention or comprehension: Humans have no memory of the future and no respect for the past. Life is short. In our haste to indulge our hedonism, feed our lusts, and preen our egos, the obvious eludes us. Contemptuous of it, stuck in a static present, we rush toward the abyss. We believe we are superior to Nature. Almost everything we create can hasten our demise. Lord of all things, we are not masters of ourselves. Instead, we are lost in the bosom of our own abundance. Ever since our metamorphosis from great apes to Homo sapiens, we have evolved into a self-destructive biological aberration doomed to extinction, the casualty of our own greed, arrogance, and apathy.

There is general agreement among philosophers and scientists that time is constant. But continuity does not necessarily suggest *motion*, (*i.e.*, we do not experience it as stopping and starting, or darting about at random. Some of the novel ideas from modern physics have also generated new insights and hypotheses concerning the nature of time. Philosophers keep splitting hair: Is time real or illusive, linear, or circular? But a whole host of other philosophical questions have since surfaced: Is time *tensed* or *tenseless* (conjugable)? Is the present a series of fused, instantaneous moments or does it undergo a *duration*? Can past and future be said to really exist—the former revived by memory, the latter glimpsed through the lens of imagination (or otherworldly dreams)?*

Prehistoric humans hunted, grew plants, and raised animals to survive. There was little incentive to understand time, let alone measure it. They first recorded the phases of the Moon some 30,000 years ago. Keeping track of time with sundials, water clocks, hourglasses, and mechanical devices is the way humans observed the heavens and recorded the progress (or decadence) of civilization. There is no reason to believe that they lent it an allegorical or supernatural significance.

---

* What can be inferred from *"memory of the future"* is the nagging hunch that somewhere deep in the brain's forest of neurons resides a vestigial nexus that allows us to evoke the future, to divine it, to extract from murky instinct what reason impels us to deduce. Alas, this faculty is subconsciously suppressed to defend against what we know—but refuse to acknowledge—to be the inevitable repetition of the past.

We don't all process reality the same way. We all conceive of time differently. Events deemed past in one frame of reference must be deemed future in other frames, indicating that the distinction between past and future is subjective. This is called a static view of time. In opposition stands the dynamic view of time, traceable back to Aristotle (384–322 BC) and before him to Heraclitus (circa 500 BC). By this account, the future lacks the reality of the past and present, and indeed reality is continually being added to as time passes. Ambiguity and contradiction are part of the human experience. We are the product of our genes, the artefact of our epoch, the cumulative consequence of our schooling, the guinea pigs of our social milieu, and the end-product of the cultural pressures to which we have been subjected and which made us who/what we are. *Reality* is what the *self* perceives. This singularity explains why we can observe the same phenomenon and draw different, if not contradictory, conclusions. That said, it is prudent not to become enslaved by fixed ideas under the pretext that we're entitled to disregard the truths that overwhelm us. In my world, time has no meaning. When I look at a picture of me at 26 and then discover the face of an 86-year-old man in the mirror, I do not see time at work. I see the predictable aftermath of decay, the culmination of the entropic process by which everything, from the humble single-celled protozoan to the mightiest empire, to a supernova is born and perishes. My eccentricity might be incomprehensible to those who, slaves of time, live by the clock. I only wear a watch when I venture out into an alien universe of artificial social conventions and time constraints — deadlines and the slavery of punctuality.

Back home I take it off. I don't see time as *passing*. I don't think I ever did. I see it as a distraction from the delights of not living by other people's clocks, the freedom of not giving a damn. Time is little more than a metaphor, a figure of speech, an inadequate guide to ultimate reality which leads us astray. I'm retired. But that's another story.

All animals except humans live in a recurrent present, with no sense of the temporal distinctions of past, present, and future. From time immemorial, philosophers and theologians have speculated on the true nature of time. Does time have substance and, if so, what is it made of? How do we know that time really exists? Does time have a beginning and an end? Is it a straight line, a dotted line or a circle? In fact, time doesn't go anywhere. It's a static dimension. It is we who traverse it. We invented timepieces to keep track of our own impermanence. But ponder this: What happens to time when the last clock on earth stops ticking? I hate to contradict physicists, but as I see it, time has an intrinsic existence only if there's someone around to measure it. Yes, physicists define time as the progression of events from the past to the present and beyond. But what is time in the absence of events? If a system is unchanging, it is time-*less*—not marked by time? The question, *"If a tree falls in a forest and no one is around to hear it, does it make a sound?"* is pointless. Can something exist without being perceived by consciousness? Maybe, but so what?

Time flees at a dizzying speed, taking with it the unforeseeable and the unmanageable. *"Time,"* said someone, *"prevents everything from being granted all at once."* No doubt the witticism of a philosopher ... or a jokester. Time is a thief. It takes back everything it grants, itself included.

Of course, our knowledge of the as-yet-unknowable will increase ... to the dismay and detriment of those who would keep it entombed ... like the peddlers of religion. Wouldn't it be useful if humankind dumped *"god"* in the dustbin of superstition and turned to humanism while there is still time? Or, as "time" seems to be running out, will we surrender and be swept toward perdition?

Which brings me to the final issue: There is no turning back from civilizational collapse. Collapsed societies do not bounce back. At best, having lost the unique features that typify them, they are transformed. But they do not recover.

∽≫⌒

Having spent twelve years on assignment in Central America, I am intimately acquainted with the modern-day survivors of the once formidable Mayan Empire. The empire vanished but the Maya did not. Some seven million survive — *endure* might be more accurate — scattered across Belize, Guatemala, Honduras, and Mexico. Most no longer speak the dialects of their ancestors. They are an ethnic minority whose distinctive cultural identity and heritage have been slowly eroded by the non-indigenous political and cultural interlopers who supplanted them. The precise dynamics involved in the Mayan empire's sudden and staggering downfall, one of the greatest unsolved mysteries in archaeology, are still under study. What is known is that between the 7th and

9th century, famine, brought on by deforestation, over-cultivation, a bloated, nepotistic bureaucracy, outbreaks of disease, and widespread discontent with an increasingly remote, self-absorbed and corrupt political leadership, led to massive economic failure, crippling social chaos, and internecine wars. In fact, the once mighty Maya were already in a state of rout when the first conquistadors, wielding swords in one hand and the Cross in the other, disembarked on the coast of Yucatan in 1502.

The survivors have since been reduced to servitude and forced assimilation or altering states of neglect and violent repression by the despots who now occupy and rule their ancient domain. Like the other Mesoamerican indigenous minorities, they remain suspended between two contrasting and incongruous worlds—ancient (but intimate) and modern (but alien and menacing),

Other than silent, gloomy temples, ghostly statuary, clay tablets inscribed with cuneiform script, and necropolises attesting to their existence, Sumer, ancient Egypt, classical Greece and Rome are distant phantoms of the formidable Sumerian, Pharaonic, Athenian and Roman empires. And some, like the Anasazi, Assyrians, Etruscans, Olmec, Rapa Nui of Easter Island, the inhabitants of Lost City of Petra, the Mongols, Persians, and Minoans all vanished without a trace. Eroded by wars, corruption, nepotism, unsustainable population growth, and severe food shortages, the splendor of the Ottoman Empire was followed by a slow and arduous decline that spanned less than four centuries. Once spread across three continents, its decimated pan-Islamist fragments have since been reduced to economically unstable, culturally fractured, "developing" states. Everything, EVERYTHING, atrophies from a state of plenty to a state of dearth and dissolution, from order to chaos, from peace to war, health to decrepitude, from life to death. Nothing escapes this process. Not empires, not the works and monuments of man, not nature: Mountains erode and crumble, waterways flood or dry up, the poles melt, earthquakes cleave the Earth's crust, continents split apart, nor the cosmos which is itself in a state of slow but steady decay and will eventually implode, and last, not Homo sapiens whose primal innocence, corrupted and betrayed by cycles of technological "innovations," turned to bestiality.

Having grown weary by dint of warning the world of its catastrophic environmental and socio-economic future while lamenting human indifference, well-meaning if self-deluded scientists are now inserting a glimmer of hope in their otherwise gloomy post-mortems. Running out of convincing arguments, they are preaching "stubborn optimism." Their long view now reassures us that, in spite of everything, life "will go on" after the collapse. Their feeble bleating, like their stern jargon-filled admonitions, are either ignored or hailed by a growing number of deranged individuals whose fascination, no, masochistic obsession with Apocalypse—they welcome it like a Second Advent—is as inexplicable as it is dumbfounding. Awareness of the fragility of life is one thing. It's quite another to rejoice in what could be our calamitous and irreversible extinction while rummaging for more evidence of its looming inevitability. Yes, I suspect it's coming—perhaps—but I have no idea when or how and I don't fixate on it. It's all tucked away in the back of my mind, like yesterday's news. I know I will die someday but, at my peril, I'm too busy living my life to give it another thought.

"Life" went on after the dinosaurs became extinct because nature, coaxed by evolution, orchestrated a steady transition at its own pace and imagination, allowing new life forms to evolve. Humans mismanage their environment. When nature deigns to grant anything, she does so without avarice. Being far more sensible than humans, she justifiably strikes back, sometimes with a vengeance, when defied or abused.

The dawn of Homo sapiens as an "improved" offshoot of the great apes suggests a gradual makeover from one species to another, both sharing huge amounts of DNA and strikingly similar anatomical features. One must be willfully blind or dimwitted to deny that we are very close cousins. But that's where the similarities end. Somewhere along the way, evolution bared its wicked sense of humor. It spawned great minds, monsters, and imbeciles, whereas unpretentious and guileless, now fated for extinction, the mischievous chimpanzees, the gentle gorillas, and self-effacing orangutans are at peace with nature and living out their now foreshortened solitary existence. Or so we surmise. We will never know how they feel about us as we obsess over money, twiddle our smart phones, elect imbeciles, and make war. When I peer into the eyes of a great ape, I see sadness, silent exasperation, unspoken pity, powerless resentment. I often toy with the notion that if animals had been granted the gift of speech, the first thing they would tell us is to go fuck ourselves. Lacking this facility, when vexed, monkeys and apes compensate by flinging excrement, a gesture that amply and eloquently communicates their frustration at a reckless relative who, mindless of the risks, cannot see the forest for the trees.

"POSHLOST" AND LEPROSY
Reeking of déjà vu

It was at that bittersweet moment when a writer takes one last look at a work he fondly struggled to finish and now hates to part with that I learned that Donald J. Trump, the petty, vulgar, smug, grotesque *poshlost** had been re-indicted** and that Florida was an incubator for leprosy. Coincidentally, and to no one's surprise, the state was also declared hostile toward people of color, immigrants, women, gays, and literati, and was the target of protests, lawsuits, and travel bans. I found the synchronicity of these events both amusing and oracular. It reeked of déjà vu. Quick to seize on what he calls the insidious rot permeating America, my old friend K.B., a tall, suave, wickedly witty, self-effacing, unapologetically freethinking Texan with a reverence for truth, had this to say:

> *"I took a short drive into the Texas hinterland to re-acquaint myself with Big Mouth's [Donald J. Trump] electorate and his phenomenal popularity, which increases with every indictment and incidence of low-class behavior. I'm surprised he hasn't sent one of his goons to murder a Democrat (he's too much of a coward to do it himself) ...*

---

* Untranslatable Russian term for a particularly banal-yet-obscene, foulmouthed-yet-evil character.

** Ninety-one federal and state indictments charged the former president with conspiring to overturn the results of the 2020 presidential election, obstructing the peaceful transfer of power, and threatening American democracy by instigating the Jan. 6, 2021, assault on the Capitol. Other charges would follow.

which would clinch his reelection. He could coast along and dispense with the hard and sweaty work of electioneering, focusing instead on grifting. But the whiner loves the campaign trail and the opportunity to be the center of attention, confident that his disciples, all in a state of euphoric idiocy, worship him and wallow in his excremental oratory like hogs."

Deconstructing the state where he was born and professes to fancy, K.B. added:

"You go out into the small towns everywhere in Texas and observe how gritty and impoverished these places are, and how fundamentalist in character. The folks love Trump because he openly engages them with double-talk, profanity, and the promise of eternal life in an America made great again ... while Joe Biden, ironically, the common man, comes across as effete and remote, stiff as a board, dismissive, impossible to relate to and worse, anchored to a problematic and incompetent vice-president. Like old Phineas (P.T.) Barnum, Trump understands that crowds like to be bamboozled, that bullshit sells best. So, he works his crowd mercilessly into oblivion. We might also note that this big slob's playbook so closely resembles P.T. Barnum's that we may actually be witnessing the phenomenon of reincarnation."

So much for America's decaying intellect. Taken abstractly, leprosy—thought to be a curse of the gods, a punishment for some monstrous transgression—can be seen as the fouling, the moral and psycho-social disfigurement of a society. A better term to describe the radical fascistization of a number of states, including Ron DeSantis' Florida and, much to K.B's dismay, Greg

Abbott's Texas, which signed legislation prohibiting any city or county in the state from passing laws requiring shade and water breaks for outdoor workers, is hard to coin.

Meanwhile, as I write, a business trade group representing 10,000 gunmakers, dealers, and other firearm firms is emerging as a rising force in the U.S. and starting to eclipse the might of the powerful but scandal-plagued National Rifle Association. Meet the National Shooting Sports Foundation (NSSF), the gun industry's right-wing and aggressive lobbying group. Its range of activities is broad but always geared to zealously preserve and extend the power of the gun industry. The NSSF is based in Newtown, Connecticut, site of the 2012 Sandy Hook Elementary School mass shooting in which 20 children and six adult staff were massacred with a Bushmaster semiautomatic rifle. I thought I'd get that out of the way before moving on.

∽≫≥

I've been reading excerpts from the copious eleven-year correspondence between Germany's literary titans, Johann Wolfgang von Goethe, and Friedrich Schiller. Their debates survey the metaphysical and esthetic ideas of their era, and advance often divergent views, notably on the French Revolution, an event whose roots and consequences are still the subject of heated debate and which I continue to applaud as it helped purge France of a bloated, self-indulgent, do-nothing absolute monarchy, a toadying aristocracy, a mercenary merchant class, and a debauched clergy.

The idealistic Schiller (1759-1805) asserted that to make use of political freedom one must first be free. He pleaded, to no avail, that King Louis XVI's head be spared. The considerably more pragmatic Goethe (1749-1832) doubted that the masses are endowed with political maturity. He did not devote much time contemplating the circumstances under which such intellectual ripeness might be cultivated. He believed that men, when galvanized politically, lose perspective of what is essential: truth, integrity, freedom, egalitarianism, justice. Worse, he argued, they look away when the common good is sacrificed at the altar of dogma and partisan politics. This crippling sabotage of the national psyche — I describe it as *"the breakdown of a nation's cognitive faculties and the dumbing down of its people"* — took on a frightening aspect when Donald J. Trump, a shady entrepreneur, pussy-grabber, bully, racist, tax-dodger, pathological liar, and narcissistic megalomaniac who coddles bloodthirsty despots, who displays open hostility toward women and minorities, who threatens to cut off funding to media outlets he deems purveyors of *"fake news,"* who intimidates journalists he calls *"enemies of the people,"* who pardons convicted criminals in exchange for unconditional loyalty, who encourages crowds of adoring philistines to beat up demonstrators, and who brags that, *"nothing would happen"* if he killed someone on Fifth Avenue ... became the de facto dictator of the now disunited states of America.

In acquitting the impeached president, the most brazenly corrupt person ever to occupy the White House, the Senate enthroned and anointed a king. His trickeries, lies, scams, malapropisms, fake patriotism, and overt threats provided an inexhaustible wellspring of both dark humor and exasperation while fueling the trance-like admiration of his worshippers, all of whom seem to be unaware (or too embarrassed to admit openly) that Trump is not only a diabolical con man, but a tyrant whose America-on-steroids campaign strategy, to work, relied on urban violence to boil over right up until Election Day, and for enough uninformed or willfully blind voters to conclude that it is spiraling into an abyss of anarchy and barbarity ... for which he is entirely to blame. Unless neutralized, everyone knows, he will make bullying, persecution, and bloody revenge the hallmarks of a second-term presidency. Like all megalomaniacs, elevating himself above his subjects, he is intent on acquiring godlike status.

A hundred senators cast judgment on Trump, but the saga of his impeachment would be put to rest when the ultimate jury—a hundred and fifty million voters—delivered a final verdict at the polls. Trumps' acquittal was a foregone conclusion. No one expected him to be removed from office as the two articles of impeachment demand (one would have been sufficient: abuse of power). But these are not normal times. The U.S. had structurally turned into an oligarchy (with racketeering layers of power and control as the supreme governing entity), as well as in the character of its immoral conduct and self-serving objectives. America's "heartland" spoke through forty-nine senators not inclined to risk their paychecks and perks by defecting from Trump, whose fury and penchant for revenge are well documented.

But that's another story worth retelling because it

speaks of a future foretold. I am reminded of what World War I hero and twice-elected French prime minister Georges Clémenceau (1841-1929), nicknamed "le Tigre," once said,

> *"America is the only nation in history which miraculously has gone directly from barbarism to degeneration without the usual interval of civilization."*

It is worth repeating, lest the wakeup call this book attempts to raise be ignored, that for every action, there is an equal and opposite reaction. For those unfamiliar with Newtonian physics, a simpler translation is that history sets the context for today *and* tomorrow; that everything up until now has set the stage for us to forge our own destinies; and that, as George Santayana famously warned, *"those who cannot remember the past are condemned to repeat it."*

ON THE EVE OF TOMORROW
Kaleidoscope

Will the world look back at 2023 as the year when humanity exposed its unwillingness to tackle a climate crisis of its own making? Unlikely, despite the constant and increasingly pressing reminders. Prof Johan Rockström, the joint director of the Potsdam Institute for Climate Impact Research in Germany, recently warned that the Earth was in uncharted territory and under siege:

> *"What we mean by this is that we may be seeing a shift in Earth's response to 250 years of escalated human pressures ... to a situation of 'payback' where Earth starts sending invoices back to the thin layer on Earth where humans live, in the form of off-the-charts extremes."*

Global warming in 2023 hit 1.48 degrees Celsius. It was the hottest year on record, propelling the world just hundredths of a degree away from a critical climate threshold.

Warming in the world's oceans also hit a new high. But scientists are now far more concerned about a long-term state of warming of 1.5 degrees. Above that threshold many of the Earth's ecosystems will struggle to adapt and summertime heat will approach the limits of human endurance and survivability. According to *Copernicus*, the European Union's climate and weather monitoring agency, the unprecedented heat in 2023 was caused primarily by human activity-driven climate change but was exacerbated by El Niño, a natural phenomenon that increases Pacific Ocean heat and typically boosts global temperatures. Human-induced warming, and not El Niño, however, was the primary driver of severe drought in the Amazon that sent rivers to record lows, required deliveries of food and drinking water to hundreds of river communities and killed dozens of endangered dolphins.

The concluding paragraph in this chapter in history is yet to be written—if anyone will be left to pen it. My inventory is far from complete. It lacks a preview of tomorrow's news, which can only be inferred from yesterday's events

❧

Ours is the most violent, dysfunctional, and catastrophe-prone epoch in Earth's history. Hostilities are raging worldwide. Global warming and violent climate abnormalities are feeding droughts, fires, floods, crop failures, famine, and death. Animal loss of habitat, human overpopulation, and unregulated urbanization are emboldening the onset of plagues, among them Ebola and novel strains of the coronavirus.

Isn't it time to stop reaching for the Moon (and Mars), pool the vast fortunes of a privileged few and address the pressing and persistent problems that now threaten the human race? Rhetorical question, of course. No one really gives a damn. Will you give up your gas-guzzling SUVs, ocean-polluting cruises, and air-poisoning intercontinental flights? Pollution from the multi-story behemoths of the sea and their flying counterparts is immense, despite claims that newer vessels and aircraft are clean and green. They're not. Princess Cruises was fined $40 million, the largest-ever for crimes involving the deliberate and illegal dumping overboard of oil contaminated waste and falsification of official logs in order to conceal the discharges. All ships are powered by heavy petroleum, a sludgy tar-like fuel that produces noxious fumes that harm not only passengers but all those in the vicinity of the ship, while greatly accelerating climate change. Estimates put the average daily fuel usage of each of these ships at 150 tons of fuel, which releases as much particulate matter into the air as one million automobiles each day! Cruise ships also devastate oceans by dumping passenger- and crew-generated raw sewage (toilets, sinks, showers, kitchen waste). A recent study by the non-governmental agency, *Friends of the Earth*, estimates that the entire industry dumps over one billion gallons of sewage yearly. In less affluent countries that are popular cruise ship destinations, however, locals will likely suffer more when vessels that fail to improve their pollution levels dock in areas reliant on tourist dollars. Comparing cruise passengers to *"a plague of locusts"* several European nations, including Croatia, Greece, Italy, The Netherlands, and Spain, are now drastically limiting the number of mega-ships they allow in their ports.

While the aviation industry is more fuel efficient, overall emissions have risen as the volume of air travel increases. In 2023 aviation emissions were 70% higher than in 2005. They are expected to rise by 300% by 2050. Aircraft engines produce gases, noise, and particulates from fossil fuel combustion, raising environmental concerns over their effects on global and local air quality. Jet airliners contribute to climate change by emitting carbon dioxide, the best understood greenhouse gas, nitrogen oxides, and heavy particulates. Nor are you expected to surrender your energy-greedy air conditioners and heating systems, to curtail your ravenous consumption of meat, to discard your pesticides, snub you giga-malls, large-screen TVs, and suicidal reproductive instincts. Not when your personal comfort is at stake.

Convulsing under rising waves of hatred, ignorance, superstition, and stupidity, plagued by mounting violence, the world still awaits salvation — from itself. Racked by poverty, despair, and ethnic strife, *emergent nations*, those dirt-poor, underdeveloped countries we derisively called the Third World, continue to be in desperate need of social justice, economic stability, and independence from their puppet-masters as they teeter on the brink of civil war or have already succumbed to it. In other parts of the world people struggle to preserve increasingly shrinking fragments of their ancestral homelands. Climate change puts arctic regions on thin ice, threatens to inundate coastal areas and engulf dozens of islands around the globe, while prairies wither and turn into dustbowls.

Embroiled in unwinnable wars, at home and abroad, the U.S. clings to the two-party system, both parties indistinguishable one from the other except for the partisanships and antipathies they inspire, both tied to corporate wealth, both intent on blocking meaningful reforms, both beholden to Wall Street, both involved in larceny against the poor.

According to the *International Rescue Committee* (IRC), the New York-based global humanitarian aid, relief, and development nongovernmental agency, countries across the globe continue to struggle with decades-long conflicts, economic turmoil, and the devastating effects of environmental pollution. The guardrails that once prevented such crises from spiraling out of control — including peace treaties, humanitarian aid, and accountability for violations of international law — have been weakened or dismantled. The human and economic costs of these crises and disasters are not equally shared. The countries on the IRC Watchlist are home to just 13% of the global population, yet they account for 90% of people in humanitarian need and 81% of the people who have been forcibly displaced. They include:

Ukraine. Russia's assault on Ukraine has sparked the world's fastest, largest displacement crisis in decades, according to the United Nations Refugee Agency, pushing the country into the IRC Watchlist for the first time since 2017. Many Ukrainians are facing winter without access to food, water, health care, and other essential supplies. The conflict also continues to have ripple effects across the world. It is likely to continue into 2024 and beyond, with Ukrainians facing increased risk of injury, illness, and death. At the front, trenches are being infested with rats and mice, reportedly spreading diseases that cause soldiers to vomit and bleed from their eyes, crippling combat capability and recreating the grisly conditions that plagued troops in the trench warfare of World War I. Russian missile strikes are leaving millions without water, electricity and heating in winter. More than six million Ukrainians have been displaced inside the country, while more than seven million have fled to other parts of Europe.

Predictable but not imminent when I began to research this book, Russia's invasion of Ukraine was a distant scenario. The horrors that would unfold, the scenes of devastation and human martyrdom copiously splattered on television were unimagined, beyond comprehension. Yet it wasn't the first time, be it cowardice or subterfuge, sham *neutrality* (what I define as a crime of indifference — aloofness further sullied by cowardice and opportunism or artifice), that the sheep are led to slaughter to shield those who might come to harm by defying the wolf. When I talk about neutrality, I don't include the qualms of a defenseless individual who fears to get involved but of nations that hide behind a façade of impartiality while engaging in questionable, if not criminal activities that threaten or weaken the efforts of those brave enough to intervene.

Sanctions, piecemeal arms shipments, and impassioned public pledges of support notwithstanding — all of which are prolonging the conflict, not ending it — Ukraine is being immolated to spare those whose moral obligation is not only to protest loudly but to intervene decisively. But that has always been and will always be the fate, in some cases the cold-blooded stratagem that causes entire civilizations to collapse. What we are witnessing on this side of the Atlantic, as "Charismatic" Christians praise *god* for calling upon Vladimir Putin to destroy Ukraine as a prelude to Armageddon and the Second Coming, is the piecemeal obliteration of a sovereign state and the methodical slaughter of thousands of its citizens.

And while these barbarities unfold and the world looks on in disbelief and horror, some of us wonder whether the wrong word, a misperceived facial expression, or a fatal miscalculation might put an end to the hostilities—and civilization as we know it. Russia's unprovoked invasion of Ukraine continues to raise the specter of open conflict between global nuclear powers. How long will the world watch it bleed? The excuse (championed by the U.S. and forced upon its European allies) that Ukraine is not a member of NATO, and that retaliating would lead to a nuclear conflagration is an obscene and indefensible pretext. When it was in its interest, the U.S. pulverized 140,000 Japanese civilians in Hiroshima, and 80,000 in Nagasaki. Tens of thousands of others died in the aftermath, of radiation poisoning and other injuries. To this day, the U.S. is the only nation that ever wielded atomic bombs. What it later did in Vietnam, Laos, and Cambodia (think Agent Orange, napalm, and massive low-altitude bombardments) is no less horrendous (but mitigated when the U.S. lost the war and American troops came home with their tails between their legs).

Haiti. Consistently ranked among the poorest and most corrupt countries in the world, Haiti makes it into the IRC Watchlist top ten as political instability and gang violence surged following the assassination of President Jovenel Moise in 2021. Armed gangs regularly take control of distribution routes, causing shortages of basic goods and fuel. Rising prices make it increasingly difficult for people to afford to buy the food they can access. Gang violence will continue to disrupt people's livelihoods and essential services. Kidnappings, rape, and killings are all rising, putting thousands at risk. Haiti also recorded alarming levels of food insecurity in 2023, which is expected to worsen. Humanitarian actors and other service providers will continue to face disruptions to their work, preventing aid from reaching those most affected. Meanwhile climate shocks and the first cholera outbreak in three years strain critical health and sanitation systems.

Burkina Faso. The situation in this landlocked west African nation formerly known as the Republic of Upper Volta grows increasingly dire as armed Islamist terrorist groups intensify their attacks and seize land. Tensions among the country's political factions have contributed to the instability. Members of the armed forces seized power twice in 2022. A surge in the number of vigilante groups has added to the violence. Armed groups now control as much as 40% of the country. While needs are dire, humanitarian aid is limited by conflict and lack of funding. Some towns in northern Burkina Faso are almost entirely cut off. The price of food has increased by 30%, among the highest food inflation rates in the world.

South Sudan. One of the world's least developed nations, South Sudan is still recovering from a civil war that ended in 2018. While conflict has decreased, localized fighting and human rights violations are widespread. Climate disasters including severe floods and droughts make it increasingly difficult for people to access food and basic resources. More South Sudanese people than ever before—7.8 million—are expected to face crisis levels of food insecurity in 2024 and beyond. Despite severe flooding, destroyed crops and disease outbreaks, funding shortages forced the World Food Program to suspend part of its food aid. Conflict across the country also threatens civilians and humanitarian supporters. South

Sudan consistently has the world's highest level of violence against aid workers, hindering their ability to reach people in need.

Syria. Over a decade of war has destroyed Syria's health system and left the country on the brink of economic collapse. A decade of conflict in neighboring Lebanon has further increased food prices and poverty. Currently, 70% of Syrians are unable to meet their most basic needs and millions rely on humanitarian aid. Prices of goods will continue to rise. Ongoing conflict and airstrikes could force more people to flee their homes. The first cholera outbreak in a decade threatens to overwhelm Syria's health care and water systems. Since 2014, the U.N. Security Council has authorized its agencies to deliver aid from neighboring countries into Syria. This critical lifeline could be cut off for millions in the middle of winter when needs are particularly severe.

Yemen. The crisis in Yemen is deepening as an eight-year conflict between armed groups and government forces remains unresolved. While a ceasefire reduced fighting for several months, it collapsed in 2022 and failed to mitigate the economic and health consequences of the conflict. Humanitarian funding has lagged. As it stands, 80% of the population lives in extreme poverty and more than two million children are acutely malnourished. Yemen is at increased risk of violence unless a longer ceasefire agreement is reached. Localized fighting persists, making it difficult for humanitarian organizations to deliver aid to the most vulnerable. Basic goods like food and fuel will remain unaffordable for many Yemenis.

Congo. Over one hundred armed groups fight for

control in eastern Congo, fueling a crisis that has endured for decades. Citizens are often targeted. After nearly ten years of dormancy, the M23 armed group launched new offensives, forcing families to flee their homes and disrupting humanitarian aid. Major disease outbreaks, including measles, malaria, and Ebola, continue to threaten an already weak healthcare system, putting many lives at risk. Conflict remains the key concern in Congo, especially as tensions escalate and M23 seizes more land. Leaders have been accused of inciting and supporting conflict to win over constituents. Despite peacekeeping efforts, violence against aid organizations is rising.

Ethiopia. Ethiopia is heading toward its sixth consecutive failed rainy season, which could prolong a drought already affecting 24 million people. At the same time, various conflicts across the country are disrupting lives and preventing humanitarian organizations from delivering aid. While a peace deal in 2022 could hold and offer hope for an end to the conflict in Tigray, northern Ethiopia, more than 28 million remain in need of aid. The humanitarian response to the drought in Ethiopia is insufficiently funded, even more so than in East African countries facing a similar crisis. If humanitarian groups can't deliver resources in a country that is badly affected by aid funding shortfalls, Ethiopians will starve as they are hit by drought and rising food prices. If the peace deal unravels, humanitarian needs will increase even more.

Somalia. Topping the Watchlist for the first time, Ethiopia's neighbor is facing an unprecedented drought and hunger crisis. People have already lost their lives to starvation, and the country is on the brink of famine. This is no *"natural disaster."* Human-caused climate change has increased the frequency and severity of droughts. Decades of conflict have eroded Somalia's ability to respond to shocks of any kind, destroying systems and infrastructure that would have provided a guardrail against the current crisis. For instance, with its food production decimated by climate change and conflict, Somalia's dependence on imports has proved disastrous — over 90% of its wheat comes from Russia and Ukraine. Somalia, like Ethiopia, could experience its sixth consecutive failed rainy season in 2024. High global food prices driven by the war in Ukraine make it even harder for families to eat. Humanitarian organizations have limited ability to reach people in areas controlled by non-state armed groups. There are even reports of one group destroying food deliveries and poisoning water sources. Meanwhile, the humanitarian response in Somalia remains severely underfunded.

Afghanistan. It was in 330 BC that Alexander the Great, trying to conquer Afghanistan, faced his fiercest battles and greatest losses. He gave up after eight years. Various Arab caliphates, Mongols, Persians and Sikhs also led campaigns against Afghanistan. All failed. Led to believe that they needed to occupy Afghanistan as a buffer against Russia, the British attacked the wild, remote mountainous country on three separate occasions and at a devastating cost between 1838 and 1919. The Russians tried their hand three times — in 1929, 1930, and 1979 — enduring a nine-year conflict that resulted in catastrophic losses in men and materiel. Five years into the conflict the Russians were bogged down in a guerrilla war of increasing ferocity. They failed to subdue the insurgency or win acceptance by the Afghan people. Instead, Afghan resistance grew stronger and gained popular support. Fighting spread across the country. Soviet airfields, garrisons, and lines of communication, which came under increasing attack, were ultimately disabled.

A heavily redacted document released by the U.S. Directorate of Intelligence tallies Russian casualties at about 25,000, including 8,000 dead and the destruction of more than 600 helicopters, fixed-wing aircraft, and thousands of land vehicles. According to the document, the Afghan army suffered 67,000 casualties. Insurgents lost some 40,000 men, not including civilian sympathizers. The Soviet program to transform Afghanistan into a reliable client state had no impact. Efforts at media indoctrination of Afghans failed: Most Afghans are illiterate. Fleeting loyalties and sporadic truces were obtained through bribery and deception—a subterfuge the U.S. has admitted using without success.

❧

"History," said Napoleon, *"is the version of past events that people have decided to agree upon."* His vast army's debacle on the frozen steppes of Russia in 1812, history agrees, was the result of a fundamental error in judgment. A formidable juggernaut is no match against the courage, selflessness, determination, and patience of stalwart, patriotic people, no matter how militarily outnumbered they might be. In exile on the island of Elba before escaping, reconstituting an army, and taking on the Duke of Wellington at Waterloo, Napoleon quipped:

"A leader can expect to be defeated but never taken off guard."

A century later, Adolf Hitler, a talentless would-be artist and psychopath with a messiah complex who chose surprise over the prophetic nature of past events, emulated Napoleon and invaded Russia. But *"General Winter,"* the redoubtable and invincible strategist that decimated France's Imperial Army [Napoleon lost more than half a million men] made short shrift of the Führer's best troops. The mighty Wehrmacht was not equipped for winter warfare. Worse, it underestimated the bravery and fortitude of the Soviet army. Frostbite and disease caused more casualties than actual combat, and the dead and wounded numbered more than 150,000 in the first three weeks of fighting. By the end of the offensive, which was frustrated by tenacious Russian soldiers, nearly two million German soldiers had died.

America's 20-year war (2001-2021) in Afghanistan, while vastly different from the Napoleonic and German campaigns against Russia, was lost before it even began owing a dynamic common to both: The U.S. was fighting against well organized, disciplined zealots who know and control the terrain and who, like quicksilver, scatter and disappear into the innumerable chasms, furrows, and crevices that slice through their country's vast mountainous terrain. Add to a bleak lunar topography, deeply rooted religious convictions, a fanatical love of country, and an abhorrence of foreign influences which Afghans continue to regard as meddlesome and sacrilegious.

More than 2,400 U.S. soldiers lost their lives. Some

20,000 were wounded. In addition, a dozen or more Central Intelligence Agency operatives were killed. More than 1,800 civilian contractors also died. The doubling of American troops, as the war was being lost, pleased the hawks, the bankers, and the military contractors. It was seen in many quarters as a colossal mistake and yet another example of military adventurism that neither retarded nor prevented what would turn out to be an inevitable and humiliating fiasco for the U.S. A confidential trove of government documents obtained by The Washington Post reveals that senior U.S. officials failed to tell the truth about the war in Afghanistan throughout the 20-year campaign, issuing rosy reports they knew to be false and hiding evidence that the war had become unwinnable.

Afghanistan is hopelessly mired in economic collapse. While a rapid increase in aid prevented famine last winter, the root cause of the crisis persists. Ongoing efforts to engage the government and improve the economy have fallen short. Almost the entire population is now living in poverty. Heading into winter, millions of people are unable to afford basic needs, with drought and flooding decimating crops and livestock. Afghan women and girls will experience the brunt of this hardship. They remain at risk of violence and exploitation. And many are left without a voice as the government places bans on education, dress, travel, and participation in the social and political process.

Alive, Osama bin Laden was both a symbol and the muse of anti-western theology. Since his assassination, his message and his mission have inspired and galvanized

Muslim extremists around the world. It is only when the U.S. awakens from its inflated illusions of military supremacy and moral superiority, and when it sees the world through less myopic and arrogant eyes that humanity can relax long enough to chance what could have been, but will never be, the beginning of a meaningful dialogue between a nation long perceived as an imperialist meddler and the rest of the planet.

⁂

And then there's the perennial thorn in the world's hide—a persistent source of annoyance and geopolitical turmoil driven by authoritarian regimes, widespread poverty, inequality, lack of opportunities, sectarianism, and foreign intervention—once known as the Fertile Crescent, the Levant, and more insipidly, the Middle East.

Collision source. In an editorial published 25 years ago, I called for Israeli Prime Minister Benjamin Netanyahu's resignation. Describing his governance as *"myopic, truculent, and regressive,"* I lamented the expansion of settlements in occupied areas of Palestine and petitioned for the immediate cessation to the expropriation of Arab lands, a practice condemned by the international community and seen as an invitation to unrest and violence. I also denounced his scandalous dalliance with religious zealots in Brooklyn and Jerusalem, a liaison designed to force a theocracy on a largely secular society. I decried his habit of scuttling peace negotiations and his scorn of world censure. In short, Netanyahu's regime, I asserted, was a calamity and a recipe for disaster. Roundly denounced, my views would be validated by ensuing events. Netanyahu's stern governance brought not one iota of security—perceived or actual. Instead, as successive political crises between his administration and the Palestinian leadership deepened, Jews and Arabs found themselves mired in endless conflict. Bitterness and rancor deepened with every stroke of Netanyahu's ministerial pen, every hostile decree, every broken word, every rubber bullet fired at stone-throwing youths.

Twenty-five bloodstained years later, Netanyahu, who would be reelected to an unprecedented sixth term amid charges of fraud, breach of trust, and bribery, is pushing Israel on a new collision course with the Palestinians and its steadfast and forbearing American ally. His ghoulish hatred of Palestinians has invigorated the religious Right, whose enormous financial resources and gluttonous territorial expansionist objectives are now the hallmarks of Israel's apartheid policies. Issued from the sword and resting on some of the Bible's less than endearing exhortations, these strategies have daunted attempts to bring about stability and peace.

Netanyahu, whose odium for the Palestinians is well documented, never intended to make peace. His actions and words demonstrate that his administration, from the beginning, was hell-bent on breaking the spirit of the Palestinian people. It was all smoke and mirrors.

As I write, I am reminded of what a hawkish bureaucrat at Israel's Consulate General in New York, where I worked for a time as a press attaché, said at a staff briefing on the prospects of peace. I did not know at the time whether he was stating policy or relishing a moment of wishful thinking:

"It is not in Israel's strategic interests to make peace with the Palestinians. To ensure Israel's hard-fought hegemony, we have no choice but to weaken the resolve of Palestinians by attrition, provocation, psychological warfare, the expropriation and colonization of occupied parcels of land and, ultimately, the absorption of Palestinians into a one-nation Jewish state."

I resigned a few days later. Israel's subsequent stance and deeds seem to validate the bureaucrat's avowals. He was echoing the same Zionist mantra recited privately by David Ben Gurion, Menachem Begin, and Golda Meir.

Nothing has changed. Israel's governing right fiercely opposes a two-state solution. Once perceived as Netanyahu's likely successor, former Justice Minister Gideon Sa'ar, declared:

"There is no two-state solution; there is at most a two-state slogan. It would be a mistake to return to the idea of establishing a Palestinian state in Judea and Samaria as a solution to the conflict."

Sic vita est.

❦

Of all the conflicts hemorrhaging the world, the one most likely to spill across the region is the bloody Israeli siege on Gaza. A growing number of Israelis believe that what began as a justifiable act of self-defense in response to the massacre of some 1,200 Israeli civilians on October 7, 2023, cannot be vindicated by killing thousands of innocent, uninvolved Palestinian men, women, and children who continue to die and be maimed under relentless, indiscriminate Israeli shelling. Others, deaf to

Palestinian suffering, face enduring collective trauma by ignoring the deadly consequences of the military operations in the Palestinian enclave.

Moreover, a sharp escalation of violence between Israel and Lebanon-based Hezbollah is fueling fears that Israel's war with Hamas in Gaza could induce other pro-Palestinian states to join the fight. Should major powers feel imperiled in the process, a regional war is likely to metastasize into a global war.

At first glance, South Africa's claim at the International Court of Justice in The Hague that Israel is engaging in a genocidal war against the Palestinians is absurd and obscene. Or is it? Sadly, given the rising number of Palestinian civilian casualties (more than 34,000 at this writing) the distinction between deliberate ethnic cleansing and the unavoidable consequences of armed combat (so-called "collateral damage") on a narrow, densely populated battlefield is blurred, with the word "genocide" — the premeditated extermination of an entire people — being trivialized by careless semantics and exploited to feed antisemitism around the world. It is becoming difficult to disentangle anti-Zionist political positions from the rebirth of anti-Semitism. But accusing all those who call themselves anti-Zionists of antisemitism is a form of culpable trivialization of antisemitism itself. Regretfully, footage of unarmed Palestinians being shot while waving white flags and scenes of starving and bloodied children only reinforces the unavoidable conclusion that crass disregard for human life, if not calculated murder, is at play in Israel's strategic calculus.

Shaken by the mounting loss of life among Israeli

soldiers and Palestinian civilians, which they claim is posing an existential threat to the country, more than forty senior former Israeli national security officials, celebrated scientists, and prominent business leaders sent a letter to Israel's president and speaker of parliament demanding that Netanyahu be removed from office. Signers include four former heads of Shin Bet and Mossad, Israel's domestic and foreign security agencies, two former Israel Defense Forces generals and three Nobel Prize laureates. The letter accuses Netanyahu of creating the most right-wing government ever in Israel, along with his highly controversial efforts to overhaul Israel's judiciary which they say led to security lapses that resulted in the October 7, 2023, attacks, the deadliest day in Israel's 76 years' existence.

⚭

All rivers spring from a source. All events have an origin. And every event sets off a cascade of unforeseen consequences. The process is unceasing, and the permutations are endless. In apprehending these verities, we are taught a lesson that is both axiomatic and unlearnable: All events are related. None occurs in a vacuum.

From apocalyptic weather fluctuations to devastating violence to groundbreaking conversations on artificial intelligence and gender identity, 2024 is a year of halfway points, turning points, and pointed setbacks as the world grapples with a series of cascading challenges that pushed millions of people into poverty and hunger. Ongoing and new outbreaks of violence destroyed lives and homes, displaced millions, and further divided an already polarized planet. Meanwhile, humanitarian agencies struggle to keep up. This year also proved that the era of *global boiling* has arrived, as United Nations Secretary-General António Guterres warned,

> *"Climate change is here. It is terrifying. And it is just the beginning."*

These phenomena are symptomatic and predictive of the catastrophic events that, according to German polymath Oswald Spengler (1880-1936) are pushing societies toward *"pre-death emergencies"* followed by centuries of despotism before their final collapse. Spengler had aptly likened human cultures and civilizations to biological entities, each with a limited, predictable, and deterministic lifespan. I cannot objectively look at the turmoil now mutilating the world without glimpsing a very ugly end.

It is always tempting to attribute the dirty deeds that men do to conspiracies. The truth is more banal — a rerun of human nature in the context of unfolding history: Gargantuan egos, unfettered ambition. Greed, larceny, a thirst for conquest, a longing for domination, subjugation, supremacy, stealing from the poor to enrich the hyper-wealthy, ruthless soldiers crowning themselves king, sultan, tsar, caudillo, dictator, president-for-life. Clever accountants becoming bankers; cunning lawyers running for office to subvert the law, not uphold it; dumb paper pushers telling doctors how to practice medicine; flag-waving cadets aspiring to field command; diminutive corporals dreaming of empire. What is being replayed is not some dastardly cabal by a chosen few to rule the world. They rule it already. They always did. They always will. Feudal lords controlled their vassals' lives;

slave-owners—their chattels'. In theocratic states, *"spiritual leaders"* and the *"morality brigades"* regulate men's destinies. In totalitarian states, it's the secret police and the gulags. That's adaptive evolution. Strong-willed, imaginative, ruthless men always claw their way to the top. Others fall by the wayside.

Life itself is a conspiratorial biogenic process, some of it at the atomic level. White cells attack red cells. Malignant tumors devour healthy tissue. A change in the DNA sequence causes irreparable mutations. At the macro-politico-economic level, elites exploit and destabilize the masses. The profit motive eclipses ethics. It's in man's nature to scheme, conspire, cheat and, if need be, to kill. Large dinosaurs ate small dinosaurs. Big fish eat little fish. Powerful men make minced meat of lesser ones. Sometimes, as is the case with certain inconvenient truths, special interests strike back with conspiracy theories of their own. They assert that scientifically verifiable phenomena such as global warming and bizarre, often violent meteorological anomalies are manipulated to strengthen the argument that human activity—the wanton and persistent rape of nature—affects climate. What they fear, in fact, is that mounting evidence of man's carbon imprint on nature's delicate balance will imperil states' rights and interfere with right-wing agendas, including the self-granted entitlement to foul the environment with noxious emissions, to dump toxic wastes into rivers, lakes, and oceans, to genetically modify foodstuffs, and, because it's good for business, to retard or block the advent of environment-friendly legislation. What humans can anticipate is that before the so-called and imaginary "New World Order" digs its fangs into their jugulars, a New World *Disorder* will intervene. *Homo hominis lupus.* Man is a wolf to man--with humble apologies to the magnificent wolf. There will always be lords and lordship will always produce serfs. Some serfs will attempt to usurp their masters' powers. Some will succeed and become lords themselves. While loophole-ridden laws and influence-peddlers [lobbies and political action committees] protect the right of lords to hold on to their fiefdoms, they discriminate against the vassals in ways that perpetuate their servitude. But so long as the peons have enough to eat and their basic right to *"life, liberty, and the pursuit of happiness"* is not unduly abridged, the lords will prevail. We're headed for a feudal society consisting of an increasingly smaller group of immensely rich robber-barons and a spreading mass of galley slaves whose primary function is to keep the rich wealthy and to die in their stead on remote battlefields. Anyone lucid enough, sharp-eyed enough, honest enough to acknowledge the past could have predicted it. Some did in florid mystical sermons and tearful lamentations. Some were blunter in their assessment of the future which, to this day, calls for a cataclysmic reformation not yet in our immediate future that will reverse the order of things.

Naturally, after short periods of pointless euphoria, hungering for power, men will rise ... and the world will be right back where it started. Humanity's account—so long as humans are left to live it and record it—is like a pendulum. It swings back and forth between tenuous order and ruinous chaos, between the stagnancy of peace and the intoxicating challenges and rewards of war.

There are no lasting convictions, no immutable doctrines in human affairs, only temporary accommodations jealously shared by a privileged few whose sinister genius is to have understood that democracy is an imperfect, fragile, and ultimately self-destructive system because it tolerates, nay, invites in its very bosom, the existence and proliferation of undemocratic ideas which enable wannabe inquisitors to find and burn heretics at the stake. Man is a predatory animal and survival of the fittest is [still] the working template of our age.

Meanwhile, U.S. police forces killed over 1,000 people in 2023, making that year the deadliest for murders at the hands of law enforcement in at least a decade. That's according to data from the group *Mapping Police Violence*, which recorded an average of three people killed by police daily. That same year, 136 law enforcement officers were killed in the line of duty in 2023.

EARTHLINGS
Brutish idiots

Ideally, children should be taught that the character and evolution of civilization are determined by the past, and that the past is both memorable and ineffaceable. When it comes to augury, nothing foretells the future with greater precision than a history-conscious society. Unfortunately, instead of helping them navigate the present by the light of days gone by, the public education system, utilitarian at best, instills neither erudition nor critical thinking. A climate of ferocious anti-intellectualism is fostering what we now mourn with bitter irony (but many celebrate) as *"pride of ignorance."*

There can be no meaningful learning without the compulsion to know, with curiosity being the prime stimulant of erudition. What we learn in school is largely irrelevant. It is the gift of inquisitiveness that imparts us with true knowledge. People often immerse themselves in fairy tales. But, somehow, they're fond only of those that don't dispute their own accounts of reality, that don't threaten their ideological or emotional comfort zones. They don't bother to read between the lines. They refuse to extricate fact from cautionary tale. They allow only hints of veracity — or out-and-out lies — to color their fantasies, to stimulate their adrenal glands. They're thrilled by the oblique suggestion of danger, horror, or salaciousness so long as these enticements remain abstract, so long as they're surrogates, vicarious onlookers, not partakers. Other people's travails help legitimize their voyeurism. The tales they spin betray their narcissism. Some, born with a silver spoon in their mouth, suck on it for all it's worth.

We are all remembered (and judged) by what we utter, not what we mean. Lest we be misjudged, it is advisable to choose one's words prudently. When talking about reality, metaphors are useless. Empathy is meaningless unless it is accompanied by action. Said Maimonides:

"All the evils that men cause to each other because of certain desires, or opinions, or religious principles, are rooted in ignorance."

He added:

"Teach thy tongue to say, 'I do not know,' and thou shalt progress."

What emerges from the doctrinal struggles that cleave society is a frenzied tug-of-war between conflicting ideas. Essential truths are routinely trampled in the name of dogma. Earthlings burst with opinions. Many of our mental constructs are erected on a vast scaffolding of beliefs, inferences, and pet theories—generally someone else's. Keen on cramming dormant brain cells as effortlessly as possible, we adopt, cultivate, and blithely broadcast simplistic views of reality. We cling to them and falsely claim that they are the offspring of our own cogitations because firmly entrenched opinions spare us the burden of independent reasoning, because they shield us from what we fear the most—inconvenient truths— because make-believe keeps us warm and cozy in our self-spun ideological cocoons.

It is impossible to speak of earthlings in a pre-social state. We exist only in association with others. Sooner or later *"association"* leads to tension, friction, discord, hostility, and, *in extremis,* violence. Generally, earthlings not busy with the stark affair of surviving (900 million among us — or one in eight don't have enough to eat) fall into two camps: The well-read, open-minded, socially conscious freethinkers on one side; diehard, blinkered, unschooled, intolerant reactionaries, indulgently but mendaciously self-described *"fundamentalists"* on the other. Both differ on how they perceive reality and each other, and how they go about to influence the social order. The former believe that human nature is supple enough so that society can be gradually fine-tuned. The latter think that trying to improve humankind is senseless as its fate is in *god*'s hands. The former believe in free speech and in the right not to believe. The latter put their faith in law, order, and some form of soul-saving creed. And when the two camps face off to do battle over the one institution on which their progeny's future depends — education — they differ sharply on what constitutes useful or proper learning. The former advocate curricula that unshackle young, impressionable minds from preconceived ideas, syllabi that sharpen the imagination, stimulate inquiry and critical thinking, promote social consciousness, and endow tomorrow's electors with a firm sense of their collective rights and obligations in a participatory democracy. The latter demand instruction that instills love of deity and unconditional loyalty to the fatherland.

These dichotomies beg a broader philosophical question, one that we have been struggling to answer for eons: Who are we? What exactly is an earthling? In studying the question and in hopes of avoiding unfair or absurd inferences, I have chosen to quote from the blistering observations of some of Earth's most illustrious thinkers. Diogenes of Sinope (412-323 BC), the founder of Cynicism, said:

"Most men are within a finger's breadth of being mad. They are more curious about the meaning of dreams than about things they see when awake."

Diogenes' contemporary, Plato, remarked:

"Wise men talk because they have something to say; fools, because they have to say something."

A student of Plato, Aristotle counseled:

"Be a freethinker and don't accept everything you hear as truth. Be critical and evaluate what you believe in."

In *Leviathan*, 17th century British self-avowed materialist Thomas Hobbes describes earthlings as neither good nor bad. He sees them as creatures who crave certain things and who will resort to violence when their desires are in conflict, who naturally denigrate and compete with each other, are very easily swayed by the rhetoric of ambitious persons and think much more highly of themselves than of other people. In short, their passions magnify the value they place on their own interests, especially their near-term interests. Hobbes observed:

"If any two men want the same thing, which they cannot practically both possess, they become enemies."

The things that earthlings long for in ways that lead to disputes include material gain, self-preservation,

33

propagation, and an inordinate craving for praise, all of which bring them into a state of tension in which life, in Hobbes' memorable citation, is *"solitary, poor, nasty, brutish, and short."*

For Jean-Jacques Rousseau (1712-1768) the influential and controversial French philosopher, the corruption of earthlings began with the formation of and exposure to organized society. Rousseau sought to find a way of preserving freedom in a world where humans are increasingly — and grudgingly — dependent on one another for the satisfaction of their needs. Earthlings are compulsively driven to compete and, when doable, to outdistance and dominate each other. Their one-upmanship, their passion for gain and glory, which to Hobbes was natural, was for Rousseau the result of artificial social conventions that awakened innate neuroses, ignited vile passions, and kindled the collective fires of madness:

"The first man, who having enclosed a piece of ground, bethought himself of saying, 'this is nine,' and found people simple enough to believe him, was the real founder of civil society."

With ownership, which another Frenchman, social theorist Pierre Joseph Proudhon (1809-1865) defined as *theft*, came laws, crime, economic instability, social inequality, constabularies, armies, and wars.

Writing in *Civil Disobedience*, American naturalist and lifelong abolitionist, Henry David Thoreau (1817-1862) declared:

"There are thousands who are in opinion opposed to slavery

and to the war who yet in effect do nothing to put an end to them ... There are ninety-nine patrons of virtue to one virtuous man."

Charlie Chaplin (1889-1977), one of the most astute modern social commentators, noted:

"Man as an individual is a genius. But men in the mass form a headless monster, a great, brutish idiot that goes where prodded."

Railing against conformity, Friedrich Nietzsche (1844-1900), the formidable German philosopher who challenged the foundations of Christianity and traditional morality, noted:

"When a hundred men stand together, each of them loses his mind and gets another one."

Condemning second-hand convictions often modified to suit personal need, Leonardo da Vinci (1452-1519), the prodigy who epitomized the Renaissance's humanist ideal, exclaimed:

"The greatest deception men suffer is from their own opinions."

Saint Augustine of Hippo (354-430 CE), a towering medieval thinker whose authority and ideas came to exert an enduring influence well into the modern era, advised:

"A thinking being does not make the truth; he finds it."

Arthur Schopenhauer (1788-1860), among the first philosophers to suggest that, at its core, the universe is not a rational place, proclaimed:

"There is no Absolute, no Reason, no God, no Spirit at work

in the world; nothing but the brute, instinctive will to live."

Benedict (Baruch) Spinoza (1632-1677), one of the most important and certainly one of the most radical philosophers of the early modern period whose views inspired strongly democratic political models and who decried the pretensions of sectarian religion, wrote:

"Scripture ... when it says that god is angry with sinners ... its purpose is not to teach philosophy, nor to render men wise, but to make them obedient."

Writing in *The Prince*, Niccolo Machiavelli (1469-1527), the father of political philosophy whose musings have had a widespread and lasting impact, cautioned would-be rulers:

"Men are so simple, and so much creatures of circumstance that the deceiver will always find someone ready to be deceived."

Executed on orders of King Henry VIII, Catholic martyr, Thomas More (1478-1535) who earned a reputation as a leading humanist scholar, denounced greed and hypocrisy:

"People always talk about the public interest, but all they really care about is themselves and private property."

Born at a time of religious turmoil and cultural innovation, and one of the most important painters of the Renaissance, Flemish-born Peter Brueghel aka The Elder (1525-1569). captioned one of his engravings with the following observation:

"There is no one who does not seek his own advantage everywhere, no one who does not seek himself in all that he

does, no one who does not yearn everywhere for private gain — this one pulls, that one pulls — all have the same love of possessing."

Moses ben Maimon — Maimonides — the greatest Jewish philosopher of the medieval period and quite possibly the leading rabbinical authority of all time, author of the *Guide of the Perplexed*, a masterpiece of Jewish thought that seeks to resolve the conflict between religious and secular knowledge, and mocks astrology and superstition, angered both Jews and Christians when he proclaimed:

"I call senseless beliefs and degenerate customs diseases of humanity."

Known as the dean of American science-fiction writers, Robert Heinlein (1907-1988), bitterly concluded:

"Never underestimate the power of human stupidity."

Said English writer and dystopian philosopher, Aldous Huxley (1894-1963):

"For at least two thirds of our miseries spring from human stupidity, human malice, and those great motivators and justifiers of malice and stupidity, idealism, dogmatism and proselytizing zeal on behalf of religious and political idols."

Pondering how to become a man of genius, Bertrand Russell (1872-1970) responded:

"Ignore fact and reason, live entirely in the world of your own fantastic and myth-producing passions; do this whole-heartedly and with conviction, and you will become one of the prophets of your age."

Oscar Wilde (1854-1900), the premier wit and satirist of the Victorian era and the author of rich and dramatic portrayals of the human condition, railed:

"Conformity is the last refuge of the unimaginative."

Deploring the magnitude of human stupidity, fifth century BC Greek playwright, *"The Prince of Comedy,"* Aristophanes, grumbled:

"You cannot teach a crab to walk straight."

A century earlier, Lao Tzu, a central figure in Chinese culture and the author of the *Tao Te Ching*, which advocates humility in leadership and a restrained approach to statecraft, wryly cautioned his contemporaries:

"If you do not change direction, you risk ending up where you're heading."

Albert Camus (1913-1960), whose absurdist philosophy views the universe as irrational and meaningless, held that the only way to deal with an unfree world is to become so irrevocably free that one's very existence is an act of rebellion. He pithily summed up man's existential dilemma:

"Men are not aware of the tremendous energy they must exert just to be normal."

In his best known and pivotal work, *The Revolt of the Masses*, Spanish philosopher José Ortega y Gasset (1883-1955) rises against the *"tyranny of the majority"* and the *"collective mediocrity of the masses,"* which he believes threaten individuality and freethought, and which he accuses of suffering from *"intellectual hermetism:"*

"The average man finds himself with 'ideas' in his head but he lacks the faculty of ideation [the faculty to form ideas]. *He has no conception even of the rare atmosphere in which*

ideas live. He wishes to have opinions, but is unwilling to accept the conditions and presuppositions that underlie all opinions..."

Prolific blogger and self-described *"doomer,"* Alan Urban, summarizes man's fate:

"We're not doomed because of climate change, resource depletion, or biodiversity loss. We're doomed because human nature makes those things inevitable."

Reflecting on man's fixation with *god*, the ever-playful closet atheist, Benjamin Franklin (1706-1790), quipped:

"The way to see by Faith is to shut the Eye of Reason. Lighthouses are more helpful than churches."

And grieving man's folly, Age of Enlightenment guru, mathematician, physicist, astronomer, Isaac Newton (1642-1727) sighed:

"I can calculate the motion of heavenly bodies but not the madness of people."

❧

Madness is a non-scientific term referring to mental disorders that are so severe as to inhibit licit, socially acceptable comportment. These disorders vary greatly in character and degree. In their mildest form they express themselves as fixations, unmanageable phobias, eccentricities, and exaggerated or distorted views of otherwise ordinary events. In more acute cases, they can become the matrix from which genius or criminality springs.

There's more to madness than meets the eye. Let me count the ways in which I've seen it morph on this mawkishly dubbed *little blue marble in the sky* where madmen and criminals outnumber creative geniuses a million to one. There exist ill-defined forms of mental illness so subtle, so skillfully concealed, so utterly undetectable that they elude even those trained to recognize the myriad faces behind which they hide. They are the forms of lunacy sanctioned by a society more preoccupied with appearances than reason or virtue. Is he demented who pretends to be sane? Is he who fakes madness — insane? Is conformist behavior proof of sanity? Is a clown *crazy*? Would his antics be sanctioned outside the circus tent? He's only play-acting, you say. Aren't elected officials play-acting every time they address their constituents? What about motorists who willfully exceed the speed limit; are they clear-headed, morons or criminals? Are citizens who time after time vote into office inept or corrupt politicians under the ludicrous pretext that they're taking part in the *"democratic process"* in full possession of their faculties? Or are they imbeciles who deserve the scoundrels they help elect?

Is the soldier who fires at an enemy he cannot see but aims to kill behaving rationally or, to dilute the horror (or ease his conscience if he has any), is he pretending to be shooting blanks every time he squeezes the trigger? If not, and should he be seeking moral justification in sanctioned murder, or derive some secret thrill from it, is he demented, a sadist or just another wretched victim of military indoctrination? Was he *"normal"* when he entered boot camp and did "basic training" transform him into a killer? More than a quarter of U.S. soldiers test positive for mental syndromes, including depression, panic attacks and attention deficit hyperactivity disorder *prior* to enlistment. Nearly ten percent experience suicidal tendencies. Those who are most at risk of taking their own lives also have a record of impulsive anger, a condition known as Intermittent Explosive Disorder— more than five times the rate found in the civilian population. Can one infer from these disturbing statistics that one in four enlistees is driven by psychosis rather than *"patriotism"*?

Are boxers who pummel each other senseless--out of their minds? Do they grasp the absurd bestiality of their "sport"? Would their fights-to-the-finish seem less brutish if they didn't appear to enjoy the pain they inflict on their challengers? Aren't coaches in all the neighborhood gyms that reek of beer, pee, and sweat, where dreams of glory in the ring are rewarded with defeat, disfigurement, brain damage, insanity, misery, and premature death, accessories to crime? And aren't the fans who salivate at the prospect of blood, of a bone-crushing knockout, equally deranged?

Are we to believe that the uninvited "missionaries" who force aborigines to cover their genitals under the pretext that nudity is a sin, who force-feed their children bizarre, alien concepts, who trivialize their ancestors' culture, and who devalue their identity ... are redeemers or dangerous psychopaths? Were the *"prophets"* amateur prognosticators or devious terrorists subverted by religious zeal? Or were they bewitched conspirators blinded by such love for *god* that love turned into hatred? Soothsayers who spouted esoteric charades and confabulations; cunning schemers inclined to sow fear and disorder; dream sellers, demagogues who deconstruct reality and spread cheap imitations of a false and elusive Utopia? Were their intentions noble, or did they suffer from acute megalomania, monomania, and thanatomania, that morbid, haunting fixation with death? Wouldn't they all have been dispatched to the looney bin or labelled quacks if modern psychiatry had not spinelessly refused to see them for what they were — toxic crackpots pickled in gooey mysticism, lunatics who paint every inexplicable phenomenon as the avatar of an invisible, unknowable *"creator"*? Religious fanaticism is frequently a harbinger of insanity. Earthlings are presumptuous; they are easily induced to believe that *god* speaks to them directly, and they are apt to despise those who do not enjoy such privilege. Didn't the righteous Job, said to have lived between the 17th and 15th century BC tell self-proclaimed seers:

"All of you are charlatans."

Tune in on AM and short-wave radio frequencies and listen to the maniacal Evangelical soul-robbers who lecture listeners and fill their heads with monstrosities. Look at the transfixed masses of born-again "tongue"-speaking ghouls who sway and swing and rock, their arms outstretched toward heaven as they pray for the cleansing firestorms of hell. They believe themselves to be immortal. Are they bonkers or the unwitting casualties of self-induced hysteria?

Aren't the dream merchants and the healers and the corporate kingpins who peddle cheap imitations of paradise — insufferable psychopaths? If earthlings were judged not just on their deeds but for their secret thoughts, their dreams, their hankerings, if they were put away for their natural tendencies—or for the habits and obsessions they pick up along the way—dungeons and madhouses would be bursting at the seams. But madness is somehow less reprehensible when it festers in high places; less disgraceful when ruthless tycoons are eulogized for their *"initiative,"* their *"business savvy,"* and their fortunes, less ignoble when *"my-country-right-or wrong"* flag-wavers brush aside lies, rationalize injustice, defend sleaze and political chicanery, less revolting when illegal, immoral, and unwinnable wars that enrich bankers and cannon merchants are waged far from home in the name of *"national security;"* less detestable when freedom of thought is slammed as dissent and when all moral codes are rescinded to protect the moneyed elite?

So pray tell, who are the mad, and who are the meek who inherit the wind? In plumbing our future, it takes no time to realize that what is being demanded of us are pretense, diffidence, and conformity to a social order more likely to view as sane those who surrender their individuality and follow the crowd. To survive, blend in, we must become simpletons stripped of analytical powers and forced to affect a slavish adherence to common expectations of social and emotional normalcy. Or else we must fake idiocy lest we be accused of heresy.

Such stratagems are not optimal because they do not prevent the spawning of children who do not ask to be born. I have become acutely aware of how irresponsibly Homo sapiens is reproducing on a planet with finite and dwindling resources. There were about two billion people in the world in 1937 when I was born. There are now eight billion. (The maximum number of humans that the earth can support is estimated to be around ten billion). Such an increase is unsustainable in the long run, and we are already paying the high price of such indulgence. Statistically, few pregnancies are "planned," fewer yet in overpopulated, underdeveloped parts of the world. The prime (instinctive) objective is not to reproduce but to have sex. Imagine how few (if any) children would be born if intercourse did not offer a few seconds of fleeting ecstasy.

I got my first taste of what would become an accepted concept and stark warning when I read *The Population Bomb*, a 1968 book co-authored by Stanford University Professor Paul R. Ehrlich and his wife, Stanford senior researcher in conservation biology, Anne Ehrlich. The book, which was savagely attacked by pro-technology enthusiasts (those who greedily claim that all problems have a technological solution ...) predicted worldwide famine and other major societal upheavals and advocated immediate action to limit population growth. Fears of a "population explosion" existed in the mid-20th century baby-boom years, but the book and its authors brought the idea to an even wider audience. The catastrophic, not to say apocalyptic environmental, climatic, political, socio-economic, and cultural impact of Earth's exploding population growth—a faint and distant threat in 1968—is now in full view.

Regrettably, I concluded that no one will lift a finger to avert the looming demise of society. As for America, we are too enamored of fossil fuels, Walmart, hamburgers, deep friers and soda pop, paper plates, credit cards, cars and guns, flags, "freedom," and air-conditioning, and a self-created mythical image that includes the belief that we're freer than the rest of the world; and that the U.S. is the greatest of all democracies while it is just another empire on its way down.

Isn't it time we addressed the urgent and relentless crises that now threaten the human race? Rhetorical question, of course. I do not expect many of you to answer truthfully, if at all.

∞

I have often wondered whether the most inviolate laws of physics might be missing a key theorem, an unknown factor, an elusive value that, given our limited reasoning power, prevents us from completing that master equation — the theory of everything that fully explains and links together all physical aspects of the universe. Finding a TOE is one of the major unsolved quests in physics. Religion has further obscured the search for such unified theory by declaring *god* the Grand Architect of the Universe without further explanation. In contravention of verifiable fact, man relies on inference, hypothesis, and supposition to explain the unexplainable.

Regarding the questionable existence of "alien" civilizations, there are at least two possibilities: The reason we have not been contacted by aliens is that they do not have the means to communicate. It is sort of similar to our problem of not being able to communicate with ants. Although trillions of ants live on our planet, they communicate by chemical signals that we, regardless of our larger brains, can neither interpret nor care to understand. The more primitive the means of communication, the less we are able to communicate. I figure we have the status of an ant to a sophisticated "alien." Our means of transmission are so slow and laborious that they ["aliens"] would have no patience to hear a complete sentence ... while capable of transmitting a large portion of the entire story of their civilization. It is the same between ants and men.

The next question is whether Earthlings have anything intelligent to communicate. Here again, we have the human-ant problem. Just as humans have little interest in the daily life of an ant, so, I suspect, it is with extraterrestrials. They listen to the discourse here on Earth and quickly ascertain that it is all the daft dribble that reflects the thoughts of a rather lowly creature with a proclivity to give speeches about being great again when greatness is completely outside their grasp. The "aliens" have measured us and decided that we lead lives of quiet desperation. Anyway, our radio waves have now propagated a short distance into the surrounding space and indeed even if the aliens immediately launch a rescue effort upon detection, they are likely to find by the time they arrive our planet exhausted and abandoned, with trees rising through the asphalt and the concrete and steel wasting away into the surrounding soil. They will release a beacon into a high orbit to mark our planet as a wasteland whose radioactivity is too great to permit extended stopovers. That remains the key conundrum of the Fermi paradox: the discrepancy between the absence of conclusive evidence of advanced extraterrestrial life and the apparently high likelihood of its existence. So, where is everyone? There are a number of very simple means for a passing set of space travelers to mark our solar system as "SURVEYED. DANGER. KEEP OUT." No such beacon is to be found. One often gets the eerie sensation that we are indeed alone in the universe, that while we regard ourselves as rare, amazing, and precious, we are criminally negligent creatures who recklessly lay waste to the Eden-like garden nature has so generously bequeathed. We murder each other in wanton disdain of the utter miracle of our existence. We are living sentient beings who can marvel at the stars and be awed by quantum mechanics. We explore quarks with the most powerful accelerators and examine distant galaxies with far-reaching telescopes. From the largest to smallest elements, we discover them all. And then we kill each other without much regard for the consequences. This has led me to suspect that, perhaps, Homo sapiens is a fluke, an aberration, an unpredictable and unrepeatable oddity, that we are the serendipitous and eccentric byproduct of unexplainable and random cosmic convulsions, and that, thankfully un-replicated in the universe, we are *god*'s insufferable and unrepeatable abomination.

Yes, I know the refrain … there are *"billions upon billions"* (to borrow from Carl Sagan's ebullient exhortation) of suns and planets out there so it is mathematically seductive to propose that some have since spawned "superior" civilizations (or fantastical monsters.) Appetizing fodder for sci-fi afficionados and mystics. I don't buy it. Absurd contradictions notwithstanding, there is no evidence that the cosmic dust of which we are made seeded in similar senseless fashion other celestial bodies. I propose that the "We Are Alone" posit (until refuted empirically) has as much weight as the theoretical proposition that "man" (for lack of another term) has evolved elsewhere in the universe. The likelihood that we are an unrepeatable fluke, an absurd freak, that nothing like Homo sapiens will ever emerge again, anywhere, should elicit a collective sigh of relief. Or, as Voltaire, one of France's greatest wits often quipped,

> *"If there's life on other planets, then the earth is the Universe's insane asylum."*

We all need to hear stories. But, somehow, we're fond only of those that don't dispute our own accounts of reality, that don't threaten our ideological or emotional comfort zones. We don't bother to read between the lines. We refuse to extricate fact from cautionary tale. We allow hints of veracity — or out-and-out lies — to color our fantasies, to stimulate our adrenal glands; we're thrilled by the oblique suggestion of danger, horror, or salaciousness so long as these enticements remain abstract, so long as we're surrogates, vicarious onlookers, not partakers. Other people's stories help legitimize our voyeurism. The tales we spin betray our narcissism.

When presented with competing hypotheses about the same prediction, Ockham's Razor advises, one should prefer the one that requires the fewest assumptions.

THE TOXIC NORMALCY OF SLEAZE
In money we trust

Said Aesop (620–564 BC): *"We hang the petty thieves and appoint the great ones to public office."* No doubt familiar with Aesop, 17th century French fabulist, Jean de La Fontaine, observed:

> *"Anyone entrusted with power will abuse it if not also animated with the love of truth and virtue, no matter whether he be a prince, or one of the people."*

Corruptibility is the mother of all vices. Without it, we'd live in a fiction-like world of virtue, fairness, and justice. It is as powerful an impulse as the reproductive urge and the survival instinct. Because we're human, we're all susceptible to its siren call. Self-delusion, the deliberate perversion of reality as a hedge against the sobering effects of reason, is its commonest incarnation. People who search for (or who believe to have found) paradise are the most deluded but their fantasies are usually short-lived and harmless — except when they try to inoculate others against reality.

Also predisposed toward intellectual corruptibility are those whose conduct can be manipulated — the naïve, misinformed, gullible, ignorant, those who are disconnected from meaning-reality. They're the ones who join gangs, cults or extremist political or religious groups. Of course, we engage in self-corruption by convincing ourselves that feigning to be what our parents, teachers, spiritual leaders, employers, and the ruling class expect from us can result in small rewards or, at the very least, will protect us from censure or punishment. And then there are those who can be corrupted by money and will do anything for it—lie, cheat, betray, even kill.

In some countries, the poorest ones in particular (but by no means confined to them) corruption is the bedrock in which governance, commerce, and the social contract are fused and anchored. It's become a habitual, ritualized, institutionalized reflex. It's part of the communal fabric. People have become so inured to it from youth that they no longer recognize it for what it really is: the process of decay that causes civilizations to rot and collapse.

There is a direct correlation between how people are empowered in their societies and their leaders' propensity to circumvent or crassly violate basic covenants, to prevaricate, to be suborned and to engage in the wholesale sellout of their citizens. Where people have an unimpeded voice and where a lively civil culture thrives, those in authority cannot escape public scrutiny, let alone evade public condemnation. In contrast, in crypto-monocracies where capital and political power are confined to a small, all-powerful, often dynastic oligarchy, people have a nominal voice but no clout, especially where their vital interests are curtailed and further compromised by endemic crime, violence, and the appalling incompetence and indifference of their elected officials. The *people* just don't count. Those who protest are either ignored, their grievances lost in the murky corridors of officialdom, or they risk harassment, incarceration and, often, assassination.

We've been reduced to turning our heads and looking the other way. We overlook corruption, we tacitly condone it because doing otherwise will have grave consequences. To be perceived honest or a champion of the little guy is to stand out. Defenders of just causes, paladins, rarely die of old age.

Other dynamics prevent people from heeding their conscience. One of them is the stupefying realization that politicians, given their own venality and the tangled cabals in which they engage — often in cahoots with criminal elements (money launderers, narcotraffickers, powerbrokers, influencers) — are so inextricably ensnared in shady activities that they are unable to fix the problems they create, even if they try.

There are two types of sleaze: corruption of opportunity and corruption of necessity. Born of greed, the former is instinctive, shall we say, deeply human. The latter is ignited when, reduced to their primal state and unable to survive by any other means, good people are forced to do bad things. This synchronism is not coincidental. The poorer the nation, the wealthier the governing elite, the more capital is concentrated in fewer hands, the greater the opportunity by the leaders — and necessity by the led — to do evil. Corruption does not occur in a vacuum. It is a system of values and behavioral traits that straddle the public and private sector: the corruptible always have a corrupter they can turn to.

Any profound and meaningful remedy calls for cultural and attitudinal transformations, as well as a radical shakeup of the politico-financial structures and substructures that enable corruption and those who are most vulnerable to corruptibility. Attempts to reform behavior have invariably failed. Blame it first on the widening gap between what is understood as illegal and what is unethical, with the latter hypocritically trivialized by the profiteers, then on willful amnesia—and on greed. Writing in the Guardian, columnist George Monbiot reminds us that man is driven by:

> *"The dream of acquiring wealth, spending it conspicuously and escaping the constraints of other people's needs and demands. It is accompanied, in politics and in popular culture, by toxic myths about failure and success: wealth is the goal, regardless of how it is acquired."*

Is it any surprise that Donald Trump dangled a brazen "deal" in front of some of the top U.S. oil bosses earlier this year, proposing that they donate one billion dollars to his White House re-election campaign and vowing that once back in office he would instantly tear up Joe Biden's environmental regulations and prevent any new ones, according to a bombshell new report?

According to the Washington Post, the former president made his jaw-dropping pitch, which the paper described as *"remarkably blunt and transactional"* at a dinner at his Mar-a-Lago home and club. In front of more than 20 executives, including from Chevron, Exxon and Occidental Petroleum, Trump promised to increase oil drilling in the Gulf of Mexico, remove hurdles to drilling in the Alaskan Arctic, and reverse new rules designed to cut car pollution. He would also overturn the Biden administration's decision to pause new natural gas export permits which have been denounced as *"climate bombs."*

Trump's exhortation to the oil executives that they were wealthy enough to pour on billion dollars into his campaign war-chest, at the same time pledging a U-turn on Biden's efforts to combat the climate crisis, was swiftly denounced by environmental groups, characterizing it as:

"One billion for Trump, a devastating climate future for the rest of us."

PAST IMPERFECT
A brief history of amnesia

Some stories, to make sense, must start at the end because what happened before is either forgotten, redacted, refuted, or buried in the boneyard of revisionism. The *end* I allude to is a climax rather than a finale. It's the inevitable culmination of events whose origins and consequences can be glimpsed only through the prism of hindsight. Cyclical and repetitive, such high points imply that the past and the present are one, that endings are pregnant with embryonic beginnings, some monstrous in their deformities, each self-destined, each capable of changing the course of history.

Everything we know we learn by osmosis. We don't invent anything. Our reasoning is rarely original. We regurgitate what our parents force-feed us, what our teachers drum into our thick skulls, what the clergy sermonizes as it claims to be saving our souls, what we distill under the influence of imparted prejudice or implanted phobias, from a history we haven't lived, and from what society forces us to conform to if we don't want to be ostracized.

There was a time on Earth when kings ruled supreme, everyone a warrior, usurper, plunderer, and enslaver of men. Some were so mighty and ruthless that they convinced their subjects that their power came from *god*. Common folks also believed that kings possessed the gift of wizardry, so adept were they at coaxing them to bankroll their wildest undertakings — erecting yet another castle, conscripting destitute peasants to fight their wars, commissioning flattering portraits, marble statuary, and wall-sized tapestries depicting their heroic deeds. And the people complied while the kings amassed gold and silver and seized lands to which they had neither divine nor legal right. The past is like the preface of a book: Eager to get to the *meat* of a story, few people bother to read it. To understand man's notorious amnesia, egocentricity, and violent nature, it is useful to look over one's shoulder.

During the so-called Middle Ages, night was neither longer nor shorter than it had ever been, but it was infinitely darker, filled with impenetrable shadows, and few dared to venture into the sulfurous abyss for there, under a thick mantle of ignorance and irrational beliefs, dwelt in untold numbers the loathsome incarnations of man's most hideous fears: Fear of the unknown. Fear of change. Fear of witches, demons, ravenous incubi and insatiable succubae. Fear of temptation. Fear of *god*'s merciless tribunal. Fear of Satan and Hades and Gehenna. Fear of sin and eternal damnation.

As day slowly blanched away the blackness, only the sky dared to brighten. The monstrous visions that populated night retreated for a while, but they did not vanish. They returned at a time of their own choosing. Day scattered the gloom, but it shed no light. It was just a mirage, a hesitant and fleeting sensation on the retina, not a higher state of consciousness or wisdom. It was in the full blaze of sunlight that the real horror resumed, this time inflicted on the flesh, not dreamed, branded on the soul, not imagined. The nightmare was real, fed by collective hallucinations that would bloody the pages of history for the next four centuries. The plot that drove the saga of Earth is one of ceaseless carnage. One can only skim the surface.

In 1314, falsely accused of heresy, Jacques de Molay, the last Grand Master of the Knights Templar was burned at the stake on orders of Pope Clement V, King Philip IV's sinister *éminence grise*. Hundreds of men, women, and even children would die in an orgy of unspeakable Church-mandated violence—decapitated, garroted, cast from great heights, roasted alive, drowned, crushed to death, and crucified—that lasted well into the 18th century. The "Christ-killing," "child-murdering vectors of plagues," the Jews, were not spared.

"Maldito"—damned, accursed—is a Spanish epithet reserved at the time for Marranos, the crypto-Jews of the Iberian peninsula who, coerced or out of life-saving pragmatism born of despair, converted to Christianity in the aftermath of the pogroms of 1391. These *conversos,* as they were also called, numbered more than a hundred thousand. With them the history of the Jews entered a new phase. They were flogged, had their properties seized, were subjected to ruinous levies, forbidden to trade, often dragged to the baptismal font, and routinely executed for refusing to surrender to Jesus' loving embrace.

Hatred of the Jews, fanned a thousand years earlier by the Jew named Yeshua's followers, inspired, over two centuries, nine murderous Crusades against the *heathens*, fueled the "Holy" Inquisition, and hastened their mass expulsion. Marranos—Christianized Jews who merely professed conversion in order to avoid persecution—were highly cultured, prosperous, and influential. Arousing the envy and hostility of the populace, they were hounded and abused by bands of thugs incited by the Catholic clergy. The first in a series of riots against them broke out in Toledo in 1449, leading to pillage and murder. Goaded by two priests, the mob plundered and burned scores of Jewish homes. Another attack took place in that city in 1467. Some 1,600 dwellings were consumed. Many Marranos perished in the flames or were slain, some by hanging.

Six years later, not to be outdone, the city of Cordoba erupted in a rampage pitting Christians and Marranos. In 1473, during a religious procession, a young girl carelessly dumped the contents of a chamber pot out the window, splashing an effigy of the Virgin Mary being paraded on the street below. Hundreds joined in a strident call for revenge. The mob pounced on the Marranos, accusing them of heresy, killing hundreds, and burning their homes. Girls were raped and sexually mutilated. Men, women, and children were put to the sword. The massacre and ensuing pillage lasted three days and nights. Surviving Marranos were forcibly expelled from Cordoba. Their houses were ransacked, and their possessions were purloined. In short, Jews couldn't evade antisemitic fury even by converting.

The advent of the "Holy" Inquisition was immediately followed by an edict forcing Jews to confinement in ghettos. Issued by King Ferdinand and his wife, the "Very Catholic" Queen Isabella, the edict laid the groundwork for the deportation and exile of Spanish Jews. The decree of expulsion materially increased the number, already substantial, of those who purchased freedom and security in their ancestral homeland—Jews had been living on the Iberian peninsula for five centuries—by submitting to forced baptism.

More obsessive than the Spaniards', the hatred of the Portuguese for the Jews turned to violence in Lisbon. In 1506, a Dominican priest roused the masses and, crucifix in hand, strutted through the streets of the city, crying, *"Heresy!"* and calling on the people to exterminate both Marranos and unconverted Jews. More than five hundred were massacred and incinerated on the first day. Young and old, the living and the dead, were then dragged from their houses and thrown pell-mell onto the pyre. By the second day at least 2,000 had perished.

In 1562, foreshadowing Kristallnacht and the ensuing genocidal *Final Solution*, and to accelerate the planned slaughter of more Jews and Marranos, high-ranking Church officials decreed that they be required to wear special insignias. The yellow Star of David patch would make a comeback four hundred years later, this time accompanied by identification numbers crudely tattooed on the forearm.

Under constant threat of persecution, destitution, and death, Jews and their converted brethren took flight. Thousands went to Italy, France, Flanders, and the Netherlands. Others sailed to the New World. Many trekked to the Balkans, Greece, Poland, Romania, Ukraine, and Russia. Some settled as far as India and China. Many more returned to the "Fertile Crescent" where, centuries earlier, various tribes had coalesced to create a single nation — the Jews.

❧

We Jews won't save the future by forgetting our past. Chastening Palestinians, stealing their dunams, bulldozing their homes, razing their olive groves and fruit orchards, erecting settlements on stolen property, basely equating the legitimate criticism of Israel with anti-Semitism, and pursuing a one-state policy that will see Palestinians divested of their rights and ethnic identity will not endear us to posterity. The proposition that certain people have a right to a certain piece of land by "divine decree" is a sinister aberration, especially when that piece of land is wrested from its occupants by force of arms. Unchecked, all power lurches toward tyranny.

Meanwhile, as the Palestinians, outgunned, marginalized, strangers in their own land, struggle to preserve fragments of their shrinking patrimony, new synagogues are rising on confiscated land.

YEAR OF THE DRAGON
2024: The more things change ...

The symbolism associated with dragons varies across cultures and traditions. In the chivalric and western traditions, the dragon is a symbol of evil. In most mythologies, it is the embodiment of chaos and untamed nature. Still young at this writing, and in contrast with the Year of the Rabbit (2023), which precedes it, the Year of the Dragon (2024) is known for its enigmatic nature and ambiguous portents. Chinese geomancers agree:

> *"It's a good year to stay low-profile and humble. Stay grounded and try to save money as it's going to be a tough year."*

Sound portent in any era, especially one of alarming volatility. What ultimately transpires as the dragon dances, undulates sinuously, shudders, and gyrates, is retold in the pages that follow. Think of it as old news warmed-over to remind the smug that everything is a déjà vu.

JANUARY

Presiding over all beginnings and transitions, whether abstract or concrete, sacred or profane, Janus, the Roman divinity of duality, of time elapsed and time pending, has two faces, one turned towards the past, the other towards the future. He sees everything but like *god*, he says nothing, does nothing. Reality is a many-sided gem. It's impossible to glimpse all its facets without being blinded in the process. To see everything is to see nothing. So, we mosey along, a languid eye turned to the past, a myopic eye glancing fuzzily at the future as the rot of indifference further putrefies an ailing planet whose health we casually ignore.

SHAKE, RATTLE, AND ROLL. The year began with tremors. On January 1, a magnitude 7.5 earthquake struck Japan's Noto Peninsula. The tremors and accompanying tsunami caused extensive damage. There were more than 200 fatalities. More than 1,200 were injured across multiple prefectures, making it the deadliest earthquake in Japan since 2016. A 7.0-magnitude earthquake also struck western China near the border with Kyrgyzstan. Nearly 50 people were buried in a landslide, with eight reported dead, in south-western Yunnan province. And a magnitude 4.8 earthquake hit the northwestern region of Xinjiang. China has experienced a string of natural disasters, some after extreme weather events such as sudden heavy downpours. In September 2023, rainstorms in the southern region of Guangxi triggered a mountain landslide that killed at least seven people.

ECUADOR: IF IT SNOWS, IT'S COCAINE. A military crackdown on gangs and a 60-day state of emergency followed the interruption of a live television broadcast by gunmen, the taking of more than 200 prison staff as hostages, explosions in several cities and the kidnapping of police officers, leading to nearly 2,000 arrests. Security in Ecuador has worsened since the coronavirus pandemic, which also battered the Andean nation's economy. The number of violent deaths is expected to rise. The violence crossed into the political arena when an anti-corruption presidential candidate was assassinated. The government blames the situation on the growing reach of cocaine-trafficking gangs, which have destabilized swathes of South America. Inside Ecuador's prisons gangs have taken advantage of the state's weak control to expand their power. Prison violence has become increasingly common, resulting in hundreds of deaths in incidents authorities blame on gang battles to control jails.

CRY FOR ME ARGENTINA. To the southeast, in Argentina, feminists and their defenders are under attack. *"We are facing a witch hunt from the ultra-right,"* said author, journalist, and activist Luciana Peker, who fled Argentina after repeated attempts on her life. Argentina became the largest Latin American nation to legalize abortion in 2020, but its newly elected far-right libertarian president, Javier Milei, campaigned to overturn the law saying he would call a referendum on it if necessary. Peker retorted that feminism in Argentina has been a driving force in the struggle for women's rights across Latin America, which is why it is so important for the global libertarian ultra-right to try to discipline Argentinian women.

THERE GOES THE NEIGHBORHOOD. A venture fund and a real estate startup--both with links to far-right groups — are promoting a residential development in rural Kentucky as a haven for fellow right-wingers. The promoters have presented the planned development as an *"aligned community"* for ultra-conservatives who want to *"disappear from the cultural insanity of the broader country"* and *"spearhead the revival of the region."* The move is the latest effort by the extreme right to establish geographical enclaves, following in the footsteps of movements like the so-called *"American Redoubt,"* which encourages right-wingers to engage in *"political migration"* to areas in the interior of the Pacific northwest.

ZOMBIE VIRUSES. Humanity is facing a bizarre new pandemic threat, scientists have warned. Ancient viruses frozen in the Arctic permafrost could soon be released by Earth's warming climate and unleash a major disease outbreak. Strains of the so-called *Methuselah* microbes have already been isolated by researchers who now raise fears that a new global medical emergency could be triggered — not by an illness new to science but by a dormant disease from the distant past. The world's permafrost is thinning. The upper layers of the planet's main reserves (in Canada, Siberia, and Alaska) are melting as climate change affects the Arctic disproportionately. According to meteorologists, the region is heating up several times faster than the average rate of increase in global warming. That is allowing increases in shipping, traffic and industrial development in Siberia. Huge mining operations are being planned and are going to drive vast holes into the deep permafrost to extract oil and ores. Geneticist Jean-Michel Claverie of Aix-Marseille University warned that those operations will release vast amounts of pathogens that still thrive there. Miners will walk in and inhale the viruses. The effects could be calamitous.

SOME ALTERNATIVE! More than 100,000 people turned out across Germany this month to protest against the far-right *Alternative für Deutschland* (AfD) party, which sparked an outcry after it emerged that the party's members discussed mass deportation plans at a meeting of extremists. The protests began after it emerged AfD party members had attended meetings with neo-Nazis and other extremists to plan the mass expulsion of migrants, asylum seekers, and German citizens of foreign origin deemed to have failed to integrate. Among the participants at the talks was Martin Sellner, a leader of Austria's *Identitarian Movement*, a wacko group that subscribes to the *"great replacement"* conspiracy theory which claims that there is a plot by non-white migrants [and Jews ...] to replace Europe's *"native"* white population. To achieve "self-determination," the head of the AfD Party has also announced it is considering a Brexit-style secession from the European Union.

THE BIRDS AND THE BEES. An ancient, interdependent relationship that contributes to food systems and ecosystem stability across the globe is on the verge of collapse. According to the University of Cambridge, disappearing habitats and use of pesticides are driving the extinction of pollinator species around the world. The bees, butterflies, wasps, beetles, bats, flies, and hummingbirds that distribute pollen, vital for the reproduction of over 75 percent of food crops and flowering plants—including coffee, rapeseed, and most fruits—are visibly diminishing the world over, yet little is known of the consequences for human populations. While many flowering plants can self-pollinate, or transfer pollen between their own blossoms for seed generation and propagation, most have relied on pollinators. Now, amid declines reported in many pollinator populations, a new study on the evolution of one flower species' mating system has revealed a disturbing shift that could exacerbate the challenges faced by the plants' insect partners. According to the journal *New Phytology*, the flowers' reproductive evolution is linked to environmental changes such as habitat destruction and rapid ongoing decreases in pollinator biodiversity. The long-term consequences are described as dire.

SACRIFICIAL LAMBS. A Kenyan court has charged a doomsday cult leader and dozens of suspected accomplices with manslaughter over the deaths of more than 200 people. A self-styled pastor and 94 other suspects, including his wife, pleaded not guilty to 238 counts of manslaughter, according to court documents. The pastor was also charged with terrorism. He is alleged to have incited his disciples to starve to death in order to *"meet Jesus"* in a case that provoked horror across the world. He was arrested after bodies were discovered in a forest near the Indian Ocean. Autopsies revealed that most of the victims had died of hunger. Others, including children, appeared to have been strangled, beaten or suffocated.

APOCALYPSE NOW! Humanity faces a perilous future, marked by an explosion of disinformation turbocharged by artificial intelligence and the devastating effects of climate change. So claims a report issued by the World Economic Forum (WEF) a group that, paid to identify and manage global risks, anticipates an *"elevated chance of global catastrophes"* in the next two to ten years. The report warns of *"a global risks landscape in which progress in human development is being chipped away slowly,"* leaving states and individuals vulnerable to new and resurgent perils. Experts identified misinformation and disinformation as the most severe threats.

YOU ONLY DIE TWICE. Alabama inmate Kenneth Smith, 58, sentenced to death for his role in a 1988 murder for hire who previously survived a failed attempt to execute him by lethal injection in 2022 was put to death by nitrogen hypoxia, marking the nation's first known execution to be carried out using that method. Smith died twice, the first time in anticipation of death, the second as he convulsed violently on the gurney before expiring. Smith's confessor, the Rev. Jeff Hood, who had expressed concern that the method could be inhumane, witnessed the execution, saying it was *"the most horrible thing I've ever seen."* Experts appointed by the United Nations human rights council earlier this month cautioned that, in their view, the execution method would violate the prohibition on torture and other cruel, inhuman or degrading punishment. Mississippi and Oklahoma are the only other states to approve executions by nitrogen hypoxia.

The death penalty is one of the most controversial and hotly debated topics in the world. Proponents view it as an unpleasant, but necessary way to keep society safe from those who commit the most heinous crimes. Opponents equate it with murder--revenge, not justice-- pointing out that it does not lower crime and that many individuals are mistakenly convicted and wrongly executed. More than 70 percent of the world's countries have abolished capital punishment in law or practice. The U.S. is one of only a few countries in the Western world that still puts criminals to death.

BIG OIL, STICKY FINGERS. And lo and behold,

newly discovered documents reveal that the fossil fuel industry had intimate involvement in the inception of modern climate science, along with its warnings of the severe harm climate change will wreak, only to then publicly deny this science for decades and fund ongoing efforts to delay action on the climate crisis. Said Geoffrey Supran, an expert in historic climate disinformation at the University of Miami:

> "[The documents] *contain smoking gun proof that by at least 1954, the fossil fuel industry was on notice about the potential for its products to disrupt Earth's climate on a scale significant to human civilization."*

These findings are a startling confirmation that big oil had its finger on the pulse of academic climate science for 70 years and a reminder that it continues to do so decades later by spurning basic science.

THE TRIUMPH OF ARROGANCE. Smart politicians have one thing in common: They shamelessly exploit the witlessness or fallacious beliefs of their constituents by fabricating "facts" that have no basis in truth. I have been marveling at the silence that continues to greet House Speaker Mike Johnson's spurious allegations that the separation of church and state clause, one of America's founding principles, is a "misnomer," that what the founders really intended was to prevent government from interfering with religion, not the other way around. The Speaker spoke with a forked tongue, and no one dared to contradict him, either out of ignorance of a basic Constitutional caveat or, worse, as a means to obscure it and allow religion, as it has been doing all this time, to muscle in on the body politic. The first clause of the First

Amendment is unambiguous:

> *"Congress shall make no law respecting an establishment of religion or prohibiting the free exercise thereof."*

Wary of the dangers of theocracy, what the founders (most of them closet agnostics or atheists) were saying is: Practice your religion without hindrance but don't force it on others. Yet Speaker Johnson had the temerity to claim that the separation clause is "misunderstood." Adding imbecility to historical revisionism, he blamed Thomas Jefferson (1743-1826) for having muddied the holy waters of American Christendom by exclaiming loud and clear:

> *"Question with boldness even the existence of god because if there be one, he must approve the homage of Reason rather than that of blindfolded Fear."*

Lest he be misconstrued, Jefferson added:

> *"It does me no injury for my neighbor to say there are twenty gods or no God. It neither picks my pocket nor breaks my leg. In every country and in every age, the priest has been hostile to liberty. He is always in alliance with the despot, abetting his abuses in return for protection to his own. Erecting the 'wall of separation between church and state'... is absolutely essential in a free society."*

Not to be outdone, James Madison (1751-1836), father of the Constitution, insisted that,

> *"During almost fifteen centuries has the legal establishment of Christianity been on trial. What have been its fruits? More or less in all places, pride and indolence in the clergy, ignorance and servility in the laity; in both superstition, bigotry and persecution."*

In a letter to Plymouth Colony Governor William Bradford, Madison, added,

"Religious bondage shackles and debilitates the mind and unfits it for every noble enterprise."

By challenging these explicit and well documented views, Speaker Johnson's contentious remarks fell in line with years of efforts on his part to bring Christianity into the center of American politics. He seems to be echoing the ever fulminating, anti-intellectual Martin Luther (1483-1546) who advocated that *"reason must be destroyed in all Christians"* — reason being the antithesis and mortal enemy of blind faith. Has theocrat, young-earth creationist Johnson forgotten that Thomas Paine (1736-1809) described the Bible as a *"chronicle of wickedness that has served to corrupt and brutalize mankind"* or that John Adams (1735-1826) declared that *"This would be the best of all possible worlds if there were no religion in it."* If he has, shame on him. If he knew it all along, shame on us for failing to remind him of the facts.

NINETY SECONDS TO MIDNIGHT. Tick, tick, tick, tick. The Doomsday Clock, a symbolic countdown to human extinction, remains at 90 seconds to midnight, the closest it had been since it was established in 1947. The metaphor for the looming dangers of a civilization-threatening technological catastrophe, natural disaster or world war is the brainchild of the Bulletin of Atomic Scientists. Co-founded by Albert Einstein, the publication keeps tabs on global threats, chiefly nuclear arsenals, armed conflicts, and climatic abnormalities. Based on its findings, it determines where the clock's minute hand should rest. The nearest it is to midnight, the closer the world inches toward apocalypse. The Bulletin said various global threats influenced its decision, including: the Russia-Ukraine war and the concomitant threat of a nuclear escalation, the "horrors of modern war" in Israel and Gaza, and the lack of action on the climate crisis — with 2023 designated as the hottest year on record — which threatens "billions of lives;" the increased sophistication of genetic engineering technologies; and the dramatic advance of generative artificial intelligence, which could magnify disinformation and corrupt the global information environment, thus making it harder to solve "the larger existential challenges."

This year, the Bulletin chose not to ease up on its warnings of doomsday. Global instability, widening armed conflicts, and environmental degradation have kept the watchdog organization in a state of nervous vigilance. It is also wary of the chill between the U.S. and Russia and China, two countries bristling with nuclear and other weapons of mass destruction, both committed to first-strike options. Efforts to combat climate change have also stalled. The U.S., European Union, and Australia have all wavered in their commitments to renewable energy, and Japan has backed off promises to voluntarily reduce greenhouse gas emissions. Meanwhile, China emits more of the greenhouse gases than the two biggest carbon polluters — the U.S. and India — combined, with the rate of emissions soaring by about ten percent per year.

The dualistic nature of science and technology suggests that while they can do great things — create new sources of clean energy, help diagnose, treat, and cure diseases, enhance and lengthen life, they have been and will continue to be used for evil purposes. Humans have harnessed technology and also have been tempted and driven by it. From the time fire was discovered and harnessed, people used it to cook their food and to burn down their enemies' homes. That kind of choice persists.

The closest the clock came to midnight at the height of the cold war was 11:58 p.m. in 1953 after the first detonation of a thermonuclear warhead, a hydrogen bomb. In the early 1990s, after the optimism at the end of the cold war, the clock moved furthest away from danger and was set at 17 minutes from midnight. It has since been moving closer towards extinction. Earthlings are neither able nor willing to control their collective destinies. Greedy, hedonistic, and reckless, they are engrossed in the here-and-now of their personal lives. They will not willingly renounce war as a means of settling disputes arising from the accidental or deliberate misapplication of technology. Nor will they help ease tensions magnified by mounting doctrinal difference, obscene overpopulation, and the socio-economic upheavals they engender. Driven by a headlong freneticism, a time-shrinking haste to experience, possess, exploit, and ultimately destroy what they deem to be life's rightful rewards, they're itching for a fight and stand poised to leap into an abyss of their own creation.

Who is the clock ticking for? It ticks for you and me.

FEBRUARY

February symbolizes a period of cleansing and preparation for new beginnings. The month was named after the

Roman *Februalia,* which was a month-long festival of purification and atonement. It's a period of transition. Like all intervals, it cannot prevent what is to come.

UNHOLY INTERLOPERS. President Joe Biden issued an executive order targeting four Israeli settlers in the West Bank who are known to have attacked Palestinians in the occupied territories According to the order, which imposes financial sanctions and visa bans, settlers were involved in threats, actual acts of violence, and attempts to destroy or seize Palestinian property. The penalties aim to block the four from using the U.S. financial system and bar American citizens from dealing with them. U.S. officials said they were evaluating whether to punish others involved in attacks that have intensified during the Israel-Hamas war. Palestinian authorities say some Palestinians have been killed, and human rights groups in Israel say settlers have torched cars and attacked several small Bedouin communities, forcing evacuations. White House national security adviser Jake Sullivan said that the violence,

> *"poses a grave threat to the security and stability in the West Bank, Israel, and the Middle East region, and imperils the national security and foreign policy interests of the United States."*

Responding to the Biden administration's call for restraint, and scoffing at the accusation that he and fellow ultra-nationalist minister Itamar Ben-Gvir are promoting settler violence against Palestinians, the extreme right-wing Israeli Finance Minister, Bezalel Smotrich, hit back melodramatically:

"The 'settler violence' campaign is an anti-Semitic lie spread by Israel's enemies with the aim of discrediting the pioneer settlers and the settlement enterprise and harming them, thereby discrediting the entire State of Israel."

Smotrich lives in the village of Kedumim, in the Israeli-occupied West Bank. The settlement is considered illegal under international law. His residence was also built illegally outside the settlement proper. His mantra echoes the religious fanaticism and extremist political aims of the now-defunct terrorist Kach Party to forcibly expel Palestinians from their homeland by means of psychological warfare and domestic terror campaigns:

"Peace will only be achieved once Palestinian aspirations to establish a state are dashed."

B'Tselem, the Jerusalem-based non-profit organization whose stated goals are to document human rights violations in the Israeli-occupied Palestinian territories, says that

Israel's regime of apartheid and occupation is inextricably bound up in human rights violations. B'Tselem strives to end this regime, as that is the only way forward to a future in which human rights, democracy, liberty, and equality are ensured for all people, both Palestinian and Israeli, living between the Jordan River and the Mediterranean Sea.

ON NOTICE. The U.S. carried out strikes targeting elite Iranian forces and pro-Iranian groups in Iraq and Syria in retaliation for a drone strike in Jordan that killed three U.S. service members. The White House reported the U.S. warplanes aimed at a total of 85 targets at seven different sites — three in Iraq and four in Syria. The airstrikes lasted about thirty minutes and were declared "a success." The U.S. armed forces targeted the Islamic Revolutionary Guard Corps, the Iranian regime's ideological army, its elite Quds Force, and pro-Iranian armed groups. The U.S. Middle East Command said the sites involved command and intelligence centers, as well as drone and missile storage infrastructure belonging to Iranian militias and forces *"that enabled attacks on U.S. and coalition forces."* At least eighteen pro-Iranian fighters were killed in the strikes on eastern Syria, the Syrian Observatory for Human Rights reported. In Iraq, according to the government, sixteen people died, among them civilians.

The U.S. also struck six Houthi anti-ship cruise missiles in Yemen, one day after destroying a series of Houthi drones both in the air and on the ground, and as the Iranian-backed rebel group was readying to launch them against ships in the Red Sea. The U.S. has been going after Houthi weaponry with increasing frequency as part of an effort to disrupt attacks from the Iranian-backed rebel group on international shipping lanes in the Red Sea and the Gulf of Aden. U.S. forces shot down a total of eight drones and destroyed four more before they were launched in three separate incidents. The next day, U.S. forces struck an additional Houthi anti-ship cruise missile in Yemen. The Houthi vowed to retaliate.

Israel's military have attacked more than 3,400 Hezbollah targets in southern Lebanon and more than 50 in Syria since the war in Gaza broke out on October 7, 2023. Israel Defense Forces have been trying to stop

Hezbollah's supply chain of ammunition and missiles, which Israel alleges are being smuggled from Iran to Syria and then to Lebanon.

NO TO FASCISM. Forming a human chain in front of the Reichstag [Germany's federal parliament] and chanting anti-fascist slogans, nearly 150,000 people demonstrated in the center of Berlin against the far right, while more than 200 peaceful rallies were planned in the country. The square in front of the Reichstag, in the heart of the power district, was full of people in the middle of the day. The rallies planned in the country, as they have for several weeks, testify to the shock caused by the revelation in January by the German investigative media *Correctiv* of a meeting of extremists in Potsdam, near Berlin, where, in November, a plan for the mass expulsion of foreigners or people of foreign origin was plotted. Against a backdrop of economic slowdown and inflation, the AfD continues to rise in the polls, a few months before three important regional elections in Germany's east.

MEDIA "MALPRACTICE?" CNN is facing a backlash from its own staff over editorial policies they say have led to a regurgitation of Israeli propaganda and the censoring of Palestinians perspectives in the network's coverage of the war in Gaza. Journalists in CNN newsrooms in the U.S. and overseas say broadcasts have been skewed by management edicts and a story-approval process that has resulted in highly partial coverage of the Hamas massacre on October 7, 2023, and Israel's retaliatory attack on Gaza. Said one staffer:

"The majority of news since the war began, regardless of how accurate the initial reporting, has been skewed by a

> *systemic and institutional bias within the network toward Israel."*

Ultimately, the staffer added, CNN's coverage of the Israel-Gaza war amounts to "journalistic malpractice."

They say that journalism is the first draft of history. Indelible images of the human drama are seized then frozen in time on the printed page and replayed on the airwaves. Delivered warts and all, facts should discourage revisionists from tampering with the truth. Regrettably, for many, fact has become calumny, reality a foe, truth heresy. For those whose only loyalty is to the truth, it's a lonely world. The price for such devotion is often steep and those who are willing to pay for it never lack enemies. Are some media hurtling down the rabbit hole of stonewalling, conscious prevarication, and self-censorship? Yes. What we have are faint-hearted mainstream media beholden to advertisers; a press that meekly challenges the evisceration of civil liberties; won't protest against the enfeeblement of the middle class; won't acknowledge that a huge number of Americans barely scrape by on starvation wages; won't denounce the consolidation of wealth into ever-narrowing circles of corporate power; will condemn neither racism, the right wing's blitz against labor or the obscene cost of food and life-saving medicines, nor a dysfunctional and predatory healthcare system ranked 37th after Costa Rica, Saudi Arabia and Malta! (France is still No. 1) and can't find the words to counter the odious lies spawned and aired by the MAGA Right. The result of a glut of media-driven mythmaking, the rift between reality and reporting has ended. Widening, the credibility gap, according to

Sonoma University sociology professor, Peter Phillips,

> "[has] *turned into a literal truth emergency ... the result of phony elections, illegal preemptive wars, extraordinary rendition, torture camps, doctored intelligence, and issues that intimately impact our lives at home, from healthcare to education.*"

Phillips added:

> "*The general public knows more about Winona Ryder's shoplifting trial and the Peterson murder case than they do about the history of U.S. involvement in Afghanistan and Iraq.*"

Clearly this truth emergency stems from the failures of the Fourth Estate to serve as the first draft of history and the free and outspoken conscience of an America that is merrily sauntering down a primrose path of media-driven mythmaking. It is difficult to conceive that these evasions will cease so long as media depend on advertising revenues (and the political leanings of their backers) for their survival.

DROUGHT FUELS FIRES. More than 100 people died in forest fires that continue to ravage central Chile. Hundreds of people are still missing. Between 3,000 and 6,000 homes were destroyed. Firefighters have been battling the flames with the help of helicopters and planes. But the fires, fueled by global warming-driven droughts, are spreading rapidly

THE AGE OF CYCLONES. Hurricanes are becoming so strong due to the climate crisis that their classification should be expanded to include a Category 6 storm, raising the scale from the standard 1-to-5, according to a new study published in *Proceedings of the National Academy of Sciences*. Over the past decade, five storms would have been classed at this new Category 6 strength, researchers said, which would include all hurricanes with sustained winds of 192 miles per hour or higher. Such mega-hurricanes are becoming more likely due to global warming of the oceans and atmosphere. While the number of hurricanes is not rising, researchers have found that the intensity of major storms has markedly increased during the four-decade satellite record of hurricanes. A super-heated ocean is providing extra energy to rapidly intensify hurricanes, aided by a warmer, moisture-laden atmosphere.

THE VANISHING ARAL SEA. Once the lifeblood for the thousands living around it, the Aral Sea has nearly vanished. Decades ago, deep blue and filled with fish, it was one of the world's largest inland bodies of water. It's shrunk to less than a quarter of its former size. Much of its early demise is due to human engineering and agricultural projects gone awry, now paired with climate change. Summers are hotter and longer; winters are shorter and bitterly cold. Water is harder to find, with salinity too high for plants to properly grow. For decades, the Aral—fed by rivers relying heavily on glacial melt, and intersecting the landlocked countries of Kazakhstan, Kyrgyzstan, Tajikistan, Turkmenistan, and Uzbekistan—held big fish caught and shipped across the Soviet Union. The region prospered, and thousands of migrants from across Asia and Europe moved to the Aral's shores to take jobs in canning factories. Today, the few remaining towns sit quietly along the former seabed of the Aral, technically classified as a lake, due to its lack of a direct outlet to the ocean, though residents and officials still call it a sea. Dust storms whip through, and rusted ships sit in the desert.

DEATH IN THE ARCTIC. Vladimir Putin knows only one way of dealing with those who oppose him: death, which he is sowing on an even larger scale in his war with Ukraine. Wherever he was, at liberty or in prison, hospitalized or in good health, at home or abroad, Alexei Navalny's existence had become intolerable for Vladimir Putin. Navalny had survived a poisoning attempt in 2020. When he returned to his country after months of recovery in Germany, he knew he would end up in prison. The death of Russia's most famous opposition figure at the age of 47 in an Arctic prison, announced on February 16 by the prison administration, reveals the Kremlin's determination to suppress all forms of opposition, even in their most constrained state.

ON "COMMUNISM." Kindergartners in Florida might soon be compelled to balance learning their ABCs with lectures on the history of "communism," if a Republican proposal moving through the state's legislature becomes law. House bill 1349 would also create a *"history of communism taskforce,"* hand-picked by Republican governor, Ron DeSantis, to recommend how the subject is presented in classrooms from elementary to high school starting in 2026.

DeSantis' extreme right-wing *"blueprint for America,"* a manifesto that reviles erudition and intellectualism, targets immigrants, demeans LGBTQ individuals, debases Black Americans, scorns public health, suppresses voting rights, and opposes teaching the less than admirable elements of U.S. history — especially slavery — will require students as young as five to learn about:

> *"the atrocities committed in foreign countries under the guidance of communism, the philosophy and lineages of communist thought, including cultural Marxism, [and] the increasing threat of communism in the US and [to] our allies through the 20th century."*

Having been exposed as a child to the cruel aberrations of a system hastily and deceptively labeled "communist," I have since been in the habit of writing or uttering the term flanked by quotation marks. Sadly, given man's cupidity and narcissism, the Marxist values that could have turned humanity into a united and self-sustaining family instead of ceaselessly warring factions never left the printed page. What passed for "communism," notably in Russia, Eastern Europe, China, North Korea, Cuba, Venezuela, etc., is a heavy-handed, ruthless, tyrannical system of governance in which the individual is sacrificed at the altar of the party. The only locales where a semblance of the "communist" ideals has ever been successfully implemented are Israeli cooperatives [kibbutzim] and monasteries.

Everything is semantics. It takes scoundrels to corrupt language and idiots to lap up the lies the words suggest or conceal. What passed for "communism" hopelessly perverted the virtues the paradigm embodies. Worse, it betrayed the ideals carefully crafted in Marx's *Das Kapital*, which calls for a classless society in which the means of production and the profits therefrom are shared equally. Instead of addressing urgent social problems—inequality, poverty, injustice, corruption, hunger, and illiteracy—the "communist" crusade resorted to an apostolate of terror that belied its Utopian fantasies while claiming millions of lives. Ultimately, the rules of the game of "communism," as are the sledgehammer dictates of religion, are unenforceable because they collide with human greed and egoism. There is much to regret about the dismal perversion of "communism's" objectives. Under the brutal stewardship of misguided disciples or turncoat falsifiers, Marx's magnificent folly failed. History will have to classify this failure, which cost some 100 million lives, as one of the greatest human tragedies and a sinister joke.

Aroused and nurtured by a prevailing countercurrent of chauvinism, racism, and xenophobia, The anti-"communist" hysteria sweeping America has merged with and now feeds the ravenous aims of global fascism. Left unchecked, America's growing flirtation with totalitarianism—inspired by its racist past, reinvigorated by Donald Trump's colossal fabrications and DeSantis' stupefyingly rabble-rousing oratory—could easily transform it into the terrifying white supremacist state many of its citizens seem to crave. Much can be blamed on the evils perpetrated by fictitious "communists" in the name of an imaginary and unworkable system of governance, including the rising appeal of totalitarianism in America.

❧

I was thinking. Senator Bernie Sanders, 82, who has announced his intention to run for a fourth six-year term, has been struggling during his entire career to tell it like it is, to point fingers, to expose the rascals. When he casually but justifiably, praised Fidel Castro's literacy initiatives, Trump, whose orgasmic worship of tyrants (including North Korea's Kim Jung Un, with whom he exchanged "love letters,") bared his lack of ethics, and shallow intellect by pouncing on the Vermont lawmaker, accusing him of deifying a dictator and … flirting with "communism."

For a brief, exhilarating moment, there was hope. Sanders had astutely deconstructed the arcane acrobatics that drive American politics and done his best to help fuse the Left's nebulous yearning for progressive values and substantive social reforms. He failed, not because such ideals are unsound or immoral, but because they cannot germinate, let alone flourish in America while capitalism, this country's ethos and driving force, endows a minority with unlimited power and wealth to perpetuity. Sanders wanted to put a soul back into a nation that lost its heart, that idolizes weirdoes who talk about walls, watchtowers, weapons, and wars, who pledge to repeal vital social safety nets, who push for restrictive voting laws that disenfranchise minorities, and who are all atwitter at the prospect of turning back the clock and obliterating the vestiges of New Deal reforms.

Sander's dream is no idle fantasy; it's a reminder of what a real democracy must strive for. Given the current political climate and America's pathological fear of Socialism, I am not optimistic. Many Americans will continue to vote against their interests because the only system that can lift them out of poverty and deliver equal justice is called Socialism—the system that gave us Social Security, the five-day, 40-hour work week, paid vacations, unemployment insurance, the right to unionize, workmen's compensation, the right to arbitration, etc.

In America, being called a lefty, progressive, socialist, "communist," "red," "pinko," is politically the kiss of death. It is the ultimate insult, a stain on one's character that skittish Americans—even some Liberals—will not tolerate. Sanders is unabashedly an old-school socialist, an honorable stance that has cost him dearly, including his presidential aspirations. Americans would rather elect a crook or a madman (a diabolical megalomaniac in Trump's case) than a defender of democracy. Of course, the U.S. is not the only country going berserk. Other nations are now steadily erecting temples to fascism and intolerance. If Sanders keeps adding a cautious but ineffective note of optimism to his polemics, it's in the pointless hope that some measure of reason might inspire an intellectual revolution in a country that now takes pride in its ignorance. I would have voted for him with my eyes closed had he been nominated. He killed his chances by telling truths no one wanted to hear. In America, once you attack capitalism, mercantilism, binge consumerism, racism, and religious fanaticism, you're poison.

~~~~~

Unless DeSantis' proposed curriculum unambiguously teaches that while the crimes committed in its name are real, "communism," per se, never existed, House bill 1349 will be seen as a crass attempt to brainwash young, impressionable minds. I can almost hear it:

"Now, children, being the antithesis of "communism," capitalism is not only patriotic but god's path to virtue and

immortal life."

You can call a chihuahua a descendant of the wolf but it's a stretch.

MIGHT MAKES RIGHT. The world has entered and is wading knee-deep in an era of increasing instability as countries around the globe boost military spending in response to Russia's invasion of Ukraine, the Hamas attack on Israel, Israel's lightning and massive retaliation, and China's growing assertiveness in the South China Sea. That's the conclusion of a new report released by the London-based International Institute for Strategic Studies, which also highlighted rising tensions in the Arctic, North Korea's pursuit of nuclear weapons and the rise of military regimes in the Sahel region of Africa as contributing to a *"deteriorating security environment."* The think tank, which has compiled its annual estimate of the global military situation for sixty-five years, noted:

> *"The current military-security situation heralds what is likely to be a more dangerous decade, characterized by the brazen application by some of military power to pursue claims — evoking a 'might is right' approach — as well as the desire among like-minded democracies for stronger bilateral and multilateral defense ties in response."*

Global defense spending rose nine percent to $2.2 trillion last year as Russia's full-scale invasion of Ukraine, now entering its third year, heightened concerns that China and other militarily powerful states could try to impose their will on neighbors.

TERMINAL STUPIDITY. Nearly 15 percent of Americans don't believe global warming and concomitant climate change are real, a new study out of the University of Michigan reveals. Predictably, denialism is highest in the mountain, central, and southern states, with Republican voters found most likely to reject climate science and a growing spate of devastating climatic anomalies.

According to a Guardian survey, denialism benefits the rich. While hundreds of the world's leading climate scientists expect global temperatures to rise to at least 2.5C (4.5F) above preindustrial levels this century and causing catastrophic consequences for humanity and the planet,

> *"the anti-climate effort has been largely underwritten by conservative billionaires often working through secretive funding networks. They have displaced corporations as the prime supporters of 91 think tanks, advocacy groups and industry associations which have worked to block action on climate change."*

Almost 80% of the respondents, all from the authoritative Intergovernmental Panel on Climate Change (IPCC), foresee at least 2.5C of global heating, while almost half anticipate at least 3C (5.4F). Only 6% thought the internationally agreed 1.5C (2.7F) limit would be met. Many of the scientists envisage a "semi-dystopian" future, with famines, conflicts and mass migration, driven by heatwaves, wildfires, floods and storms of an intensity and frequency far beyond those that have already struck. Numerous experts said they had been left feeling hopeless, infuriated, and scared by the failure of governments to act despite the glaring scientific evidence provided. Said Gretta Pecl, at the University of Tasmania:

"I think we are headed for major societal disturbances within the next five years." [Authorities] *will be overwhelmed by extreme event after extreme event, food production will be disrupted. I could not feel greater despair over the future."*

Experts were clear on why the world is failing to tackle the climate crisis. A lack of political will was cited by almost three-quarters of the respondents, while 60% also blamed vested corporate interests, such as the fossil fuel industry.

SPERMICIDE? The marriage between right-wing politics and religion produces monsters The end of Roe inevitably accelerated efforts to invade people's privacy and feloniously punish them for their abortions, stillbirths, and miscarriages. A grotesque ruling by the Alabama Supreme Court that in-vitro fertilized embryos are *'extrauterine children'* literally criminalizes standard medical care. Physicians are reacting with shock and fury to a decision that has shut down in vitro fertilization at the state's largest infertility clinics. The depravity of this edict is so seductive that several states are now contemplating its adoption. The ruling is a reminder of how important "fetal *personhood*" has become for both the Church-led antiabortion movement and the Republican Party—and of its potentially drastic consequences. In the U.S. today, recognizing the value of an embryo or fetus sets a precedent that no state can permit access to abortion—and that anyone who chooses abortion is committing a crime.

Question: Under this nightmarish ruling and to quote from the Biblical injunction against the sin of *"spilling one's seed,"* (Genesis 38:9) would a man who masturbates be prosecuted for murdering his spermatozoa?

ONLY IN AMERICA. Tennessee Republican Governor Bill Lee signed a bill that allows people in the state to refuse to "solemnize," or perform a marriage if they disagree with it. The bill is absurd and patently unconstitutional. Public officials don't get to assume public office and then pick and choose which constituents to serve. GOP state Rep. Monty Fritts, who sponsored the bill, told the state Subcommittee on Children and Family Affairs that the law would allow an officiant to refuse to solemnize a marriage for

> *"reasons of conscience or other religious beliefs. As societal views change about what constitutes a marriage, officiants must be able to refuse to solemnize marriages that are contrary to their beliefs. The government has a responsibility to protect the exercise of religious beliefs. Those with the authority to perform civil ceremonies would also be permitted to refuse to solemnize marriage for reasons of conscience."*

The bill is widely seen as intended to target marriages of same-sex, interfaith, and interracial couples.

Whereupon the very next day Gov. Bill Lee signed a law that prohibits gender-affirming care for minors, the latest state to do so as part of a wider Republican-pushed effort nationwide.

IN COLD BLOOD. More than 100 Palestinians died and 280 more were injured after Israeli troops fired on a large crowd of Palestinians racing to pull food off an aid convoy in Gaza City. This brings the death toll since the start of the Israel-Hamas war to more than 30,000. The IDF claimed that most of the dead were trampled in a stampede linked to the chaos and that its troops fired at some in the crowd who they believed moved toward them in a threatening way.

Speaking in the wake of these tragic events, Audrey Sasson, director of Jews for Racial and Economic Justice, said,

"You do not have to be Arab, Muslim, Palestinian or, in my case, in the case of our members, Jews who say 'no' to speak out against an unfolding genocide. You simply need to be a human being who is paying attention."

It is this writer's conclusion that this latest massacre wasn't an isolated incident but the methodical crushing of a narrow strip of land, transformed by a freewheeling army into a field of ruins at the cost of a terrible human toll.

HIGH FEVER. Humanity is on a trajectory to experience the hottest February in history, after a record nine months of abnormal heat, according to a Berkeley Earth scientist. Zeke Hausfather said the rise in recent weeks was on course for 2C of warming above pre-industrial levels, though this should be the brief, peak impact of El Niño if it follows the path of previous years and starts to cool down in the months ahead.

PUTIN ON THE BLITZ. And so, on this leap year Thursday February 29, Russian President Vladimir Putin delivered his annual state of the nation address, issuing explicit nuclear threats to the West. He warned that if Ukraine's Western backers deepened their involvement in the war, such as sending troops, the consequences for the "invaders" would be "tragic" and would risk starting a nuclear war. The remarks came just days after French President Emmanuel Macron said Western countries should not rule out deploying ground troops in Ukraine. NATO allies, including the U.S. publicly rejected the suggestion.

JIHADIST VIOLENCE. About 170 people were "executed" in attacks on three villages in northern Burkina Faso as jihadist violence flared in the junta-ruled African nation. Survivors of the attacks said dozens of women and young children were among the dead. Burkina Faso has been grappling with a jihadist insurgency waged by rebels affiliated with al-Qaida and the Islamic State group that spilled over from neighboring Mali in 2015. The violence has killed almost 20,000 people and displaced more than two million.

MARCH

The month of March symbolizes renewal, rebirth, balance and equilibrium, cleansing and purification, fertility and creativity. That's the good news. Consistent with man's less than romantic pursuits, March is named after Mars, the god of war. And the Ides of March, a day in the ancient Roman calendar that falls on March 15, is associated with misfortune and doom, more specifically as the date on which Roman dictator Julius Caesar was assassinated in 44 BC. The incident was immortalized in Shakespeare's tragedy, *Julius Caesar,* in which a soothsayer warns the emperor to "beware the Ides of March."

During its more than 500-year existence, nearly half of Rome's 82 emperors were assassinated. Although they reigned supreme, they were endlessly embroiled in political cabals, sectarian disputes, and personal vendettas, and were often victims of calculated betrayals and the target of justifiable revenge. Given America's volatile political climate and the specter of fascism hovering in ever-widening circles, voters should think twice before surrendering the nation to some deranged, self-preening megalomaniac. The harm such tyrant would cause is incalculable. One can only hope that a sufficient number of level-headed citizens will awaken just in time from their vulgar secessionist illusions and pull the right lever on election day. It is this writer's hunch—and expectation—that, if enthroned (and following a brief period of narcissistic elation punctuated by unpardonable assaults on democracy, including paybacks, persecutions, and paranoia) such despot, having plunged the empire into chaos, will most likely be dealt with in a manner befitting his crime. Julius Caesar (100 BC-44 BC) accused of undermining the republic; Caligula (12-41 CE), for his feats of bestiality and carnage; Domitian (51–96 CE), for his cruelty, paranoia, and despotism; and Commodus (161-192 CE) a debauched and corrupt despot who viewed himself as the reincarnated Greek god, Hercules, come to mind.

ABORTION RIGHT ENSHRINED. France becomes the only country to explicitly guarantee the right to abortion in its constitution. Abortion is broadly legal across Europe, and governments have been gradually expanding abortion rights. Women can access abortion in more than 40 European nations from Portugal to Russia, with varying rules on how late in a pregnancy it is allowed. Abortion is banned or tightly restricted in ultra-Catholic Poland.

The 2022 U.S. Supreme Court decision overturning long-held abortion rights was the catalyst for the French parliament's overwhelming vote to add a constitutional amendment proclaiming,

"the freedom of women to have recourse to an abortion, which is guaranteed."

Although widely available before, abortions were legalized in France in 1974. France's National Assembly also passed a bill that gives single women and lesbian couples legal access to IVF, egg freezing, and other forms of assisted reproduction. The cost of the treatment would be completely reimbursed by the state, as long as the woman is under 43 years old. France is also considering legislation that would allow terminally ill patients whose prospects for a dignified and bearable end-of-life options have been exhausted to be euthanized. Society censures abortion and euthanasia not because they rob it of a genius or virtuoso, but because they deprive the state of a taxpayer and the Church of a hostage.

It's obscene: In America, the Church and the rightwing zealots insist on protecting a fetus at all costs. But once children are out of the womb they don't give a damn if they live, if they have enough to eat, or if they die.

STATE OF THE PRESIDENT. Well, Americans got to see and hear a Joe Biden they didn't know existed: Feisty, focused, articulate, witty, sure of himself. He received boisterous cheers and countless standing ovations during his last State of the Union address. Even some Republicans applauded. Democrats are rejoicing and hoping for a miracle coming November 5. Miracles are hard to come by when the challenger, a deranged, self-preening, power-crazy villain commands such a devastating lead.

ZIEG HEIL! To Donald Trump, ultra-fascist Hungarian strongman Viktor Orbán is *"fantastic."* Chinese leader Xi Jinping is *"brilliant."* North Korea's Kim Jong Un, with whom he boasted exchanging love letters, is *"an O.K. guy."* And, most alarmingly, he is quoted as having insisted that Adolf Hitler *"did some good things."* Sources close to the former president also quoted him as calling Vladimir Putin an *"O.K. guy,"* as saying that [the U.S.] had *"pushed North Korea into a corner,"* and that *"if we didn't have NATO, then Putin wouldn't be doing 'these' things."* Trump's lavish praise for Hungarian Prime Minister Orbán while hosting him at Mar-a-Lago this month, just days after all but sealing the Republican nomination on Super Tuesday, shows it's a worldview he's doubling down on. *"There's nobody that's better, smarter or a better leader than Viktor Orbán,"* Trump said, adding, *"He's the boss and he's a great leader, fantastic leader. In Europe and around the world, they respect him."*

HOLY GAFFE. In an unparalleled display of naïveté — or was it callous indifference, Pope Francis, commenting on the war in Ukraine, suggested that:

> *"The strongest one is the one who looks at the situation, thinks about the people and has the courage of the white flag, and negotiates."*

He did not venture to say what he would do if Russia invaded the Vatican. White flags are traditionally a symbol of surrender on the battlefield. The Lateran Treaty of 1929 declared Vatican City a neutral country in international relations. It requires the Pope to abstain from mediation unless requested by all parties. No one asked the pontiff to pontificate about the war. A Vatican spokesman later said Francis was speaking of stopping the fighting through negotiation, not capitulation. He should have said so. Ukraine wasted no time making its displeasure known. A statement by the foreign ministry noted *that,*

> *"instead of appeals that legalize the right of the strong [Russia] to disregard the norms of international law, the head of the Holy See would be expected to send signals to the world community about the need to immediately join forces to ensure the victory of good over evil, as well as appeals to the attacker, not to the victim."*

Amen.

BIBI REBUKED. U.S. Senate Majority Leader Chuck Schumer called on Israel to hold new elections, saying he believes Israeli Prime Minister Benjamin Netanyahu has *"lost his way"* and is an obstacle to peace in the region amid a growing humanitarian crisis in Gaza. Schumer, the first Jewish majority leader in the Senate and the highest-ranking Jewish official in the U.S., strongly criticized Netanyahu in a 40-minute speech on the Senate floor. Arguing that Israel cannot "survive if it becomes a pariah," and that a two-state solution is the only road to peace and security, Schumer said Netanyahu had put himself in a coalition of far-right extremists and, as a result,

> *"has been too willing to tolerate the civilian toll in Gaza, which is pushing support for Israel worldwide to historic lows."*

The high-level admonition comes as an increasing number of Democrats pushed back against Israel and as President Joe Biden has stepped up public pressure on Netanyahu's government, arguing that he needs to pay more attention to the civilian death toll in Gaza.

Five months after Israel's lightning and crushing response to the massacre of 1,200 Israeli civilians and the kidnapping of some 250 by Hamas militiamen, the narrow strip of Palestinian land is now largely uninhabitable. Without genuine pressure on Israel, no real reconstruction will be possible. It is pointless to invoke a two-state solution if this aggrieved territory remains a field of ruins. The *"Dahiya doctrine,"* an Israeli military strategy calling for the destruction of civilian infrastructure as a means of pressuring hostile regimes, is a legacy of the 2006 war between Israel and Hezbollah in Lebanon. At that time, it involved the obliteration of a district in the southern suburbs of Beirut, a stronghold of the Shiite militia. Five months after the start of Israel's retaliation in Gaza in response to the massacre of civilians by Hamas militiamen on October 7, 2023, analysis of satellite images shows that this stratagem has been methodically used in almost every town in Gaza. This unrestricted use of firepower means that the distinction between civilian and military targets has been blurred. The Israeli army has blamed the Palestinian militia for this, as its infrastructure is interwoven into the urban fabric of Gaza, one of the most densely populated territories in the world. The tactical argument is put into perspective, however, by statements from Israeli officials who openly point to another objective. Echoing the policies articulated by the Israeli Consulate bureaucrat I quoted earlier in this narrative (see page 22), Colonel Yogev Bar-Shesht, deputy head of the Civil Administration in charge of the Palestinian territories, left no doubt as to Gaza's future:

> *"Whoever returns here, if they return here after, will find scorched earth. No houses, no agriculture, no nothing. They have no future."*

According to the U.N. Goldstone fact-finding commission report, the doctrine is designed to punish, humiliate, and terrorize a civilian population. Israeli journalist Yaron London wrote in 2008 that the doctrine,

> *"will become entrenched in our security discourse."*

Princeton University Prof. Richard Falk wrote that under the doctrine,

> *"the civilian infrastructure of adversaries such as Hamas or Hezbollah are treated as permissible military targets, which is not only an overt violation of the most elementary norms of the law of war and of universal morality, but an avowal of a doctrine of violence that needs to be called by its proper name: state terrorism."*

Senator Schumer's pleas, which drew sharp criticism both in the U.S. and Israel, mirror the feelings of many in high places who lack the courage to articulate them publicly.

The civilian death toll in Gaza now stands at more

than 34,000. If a ceasefire isn't reached and fighting continues apace over the same timeframe, researchers from the Johns Hopkins University Center for Humanitarian Health and the London School of Hygiene and Tropical Medicine project between 58,000 and 67,000 excess deaths—fatalities caused directly by Israel's military or indirectly by factors like disease and restricted access to medical care or sanitation.

"ACCELERATIONISM." Or fast track to civil war. Three months into 2024, and dire predictions of political violence are now commonly circulated both by the country's extreme fringes (and feared by the mainstream). Former President Donald Trump has been perhaps the most vociferous prognosticator [and catalyst] threatening a *"bloodbath"* should the criminal charges against him lead to a 2024 election loss. So warn Bruce Hoffman, senior fellow for counterterrorism and homeland security at the Council of Foreign Relations and a professor at Georgetown University, and Jacob Ware, a research fellow at the Council of Foreign Relations and an adjunct professor at Georgetown University and DeSales University, co-authors of *"God, Guns, and Sedition: Far-Right Terrorism in America."* The book cites *"How Civil Wars Start: And How to Stop Them,"* by renowned political scientist, Barbara F. Walter, who argues that the U.S. is *"closer to civil war than any of us would like to believe."* Walter blames a toxic mix of political extremism and polarization, social and cultural tribalism, the popular embrace of conspiracy theories, proliferation of guns and well-armed militias, the erosion of faith in government and the liberal, Western democratic state. Among the key factors she cites is *accelerationism*—which Walter describes as,

> *"the apocalyptic belief that modern society is irredeemable and that its end must be hastened, so that a new order can be brought into being."*

Accelerationism is embraced by a spectrum of white supremacists, white nationalists, racists, antisemites, xenophobes, and anti-government militants as a clarion call to revolution. They believe that the modern Western, liberal state is so corrupt and inept that it must be destroyed in order to create a new society and way of governance.

It should be no surprise that among the most fervent defenders of Second Amendment rights are people who express their desire for a new civil war.

DICTATOR FOR LIFE? Vladimir Putin has ruled Russia for almost twenty-five years. He has since amended the constitution. Given the absence of independent observers, a propaganda machine that crushes dissent and silences dissidents, his re-election for a fifth presidential term this month by more than 87% of the vote was predictable. He can now extend his reign indefinitely. The three pre-approved puppet "opposition" candidates helped legitimize Putin's victory as fearless agitators continue to be imprisoned or assassinated.

Meanwhile, Donald Trump's unctuous praise and support for Putin are fueling alarm among intelligence officials and other national security experts who fear another Trump presidency will benefit Moscow and harm American democracy and interests overseas. Trump's adulation for autocrats was displayed again this month at

Mar-a-Lago, where he hosted Viktor Orbán, the fascist Hungarian prime minister who is a close Putin ally and who opposes aid to Ukraine whom Trump praised:

"There's nobody that's better, smarter or a better leader than Viktor Orbán."

Commenting on Russia's invasion of Ukraine, Trump described Putin as a *"genius"* and *"savvy."* What matters to autocrats like Putin, Orban, Xi Xing Ping, Kim Jung Un, and Donal Trump is not so much the triumph of unchallenged reelection but the orgasmic pleasure they derive in sowing fear and wresting unconditional obedience from the people. Through false ballots, they are allowed to do whatever they want with their power. Thick as thieves, birds of a feather...

MOSCOW BLOODBATH. Assailants burst into a large concert hall in Moscow on March 22, and sprayed the crowd with gunfire, killing at least 137 people, injuring more than 100, and setting fire to the venue in a brazen attack just days after President Vladimir Putin cemented his grip on power in a highly orchestrated electoral landslide. The Islamic State [ISIS} group claimed responsibility for the attack in a statement posted on affiliated channels on social media. A U.S. intelligence official said that U.S. agencies had learned the group's branch in Afghanistan was planning an attack in Moscow and shared the information with Russian officials. The attack was the deadliest in Russia in years and the latest in a long series of violent assaults during Vladimir Putin's nearly quarter-century reign.

• Over a two-week period in September 1999, four

apartment buildings were bombed in Moscow and two other cities, killing a total of 307 people. Officials blamed militants from the separatist region of Chechnya.

- About 40 Chechen militants on Oct. 23, 2002, stormed a Moscow theater, taking some 850 hostages and planting explosives in the auditorium. Russian special forces elected not to storm the theater because of its difficult layout and the presence of explosives in the hall. On the morning of the fourth day, Russian forces pumped an unidentified sleeping gas into the building's ventilation system, killing the assailants. At the same time, 132 hostages died, mostly from the effects of the gas.

- Assailants stormed a school in the Russian town of Beslan, near Chechnya, on the morning of Sept. 1, 2004, the first day of school, when many children were accompanied by their parents. The number of hostages held by the militants was estimated at about 1,100. Two days later, a severe explosion shook the building and Russian forces rushed in. When the fighting was over, 334 civilians were dead or fatally wounded, more than half of them children, along with 31 attackers.

- Russia's subways, with large numbers of people in restricted spaces, were frequent targets. A suicide bomber killed 41 people on a Moscow subway train in February 2004. Five months later, one day before the Beslan attack, a female suicide bomber blew herself up outside a Moscow subway station, killing 10 people and her accomplice; the bomb may have been intended for a train but detonated prematurely. Suicide bombings of two Moscow subway trains about 40 minutes apart in March 2010 killed about 40 people.

- In 2013, suicide bombers targeted a train station and a bus on consecutive days in Volgograd, killing 34 people. Fifteen people died in a suicide bombing in 2017 of the St. Petersburg subway, one of the world's deepest systems.

- A week before the Beslan school seizure, suicide bombers destroyed two airliners on the same night, killing 90 passengers and crew aboard. Both planes had taken off from Moscow. Suicide bombers also attacked the airport in 2011, killing 37 people.

- In 2015, a bomb blew up a Russian airliner flying tourists home from the Egyptian resort of Sharm el-Sheikh, killing all 224 passengers. The Islamic State claimed responsibility.

THE VAMPIRE STATE. Florida will have one of the country's most restrictive, not to say arbitrary and offensive social media bans for minors — if it withstands expected legal challenges — under a bill signed by Republican Florida Gov. Ron DeSantis. The bill will ban social media accounts for children under 14 and require parental permission for 15- and 16-year-olds. The new law, scheduled to take effect in 2025, was Republican Speaker Paul Renner's top legislative priority. Florida is a hot spot in the clash over what reading material is appropriate for children, with laws that have greatly expanded the state's ability to restrict books. One must question the urgency of such legislation at a time when

Florida's "anti-woke" culture wars are being waged to distract from such challenges as crass violation of individual rights (think abortions), runaway inflation, overdevelopment, overpopulation, unaffordable housing, dismal road conditions, chocking traffic, and homicidal drivers.

Predictably, several overwhelmingly conservative states experiencing the same problems are considering adopting similar legislation. [I was reading the Marquis de Sade *en français* when I was 12. What I gained in the process is an appreciation for the seductive power of in-your-face political activism cleverly posing as erotic literature. What I lost, prematurely but unrepentantly was my virginity. Mercifully, I was in France at the time, a nation that doesn't tell its citizens what they can and cannot read].*

BRIDGE OVER TROUBLED WATERS. Baltimore's Francis Scott Key Bridge collapsed after a container ship lost power and rammed into the span, sending vehicles plunging into the water. The ship reported losing power just before it struck a column on the bridge, authorities said. Two people were pulled from the water following the collapse; one was in serious condition. Four people are still unaccounted for. Rescuers are searching for six

---

* The French patronize independent bookstores and are inextricably tied to the literary output of the country. Last year, 150 bookstores opened in France. There are currently 3,500 independent bookstores across France. These shops feature novels and political texts, comics, and children's books. The government has given independent bookstores considerable protection from larger competitors, including Amazon. No country hosts more book fairs each year than France.

construction workers who were working on the bridge at the time of the collapse. No sooner did the span break apart like a disarticulated erector set than conspiracy theories, one more fantastical than the other, began to circulate. Claims ranged from a cyber-attack or a ship captain impaired by side effects from Covid-19 vaccines to accusations that Israel, or even the Obamas had something to do with the bridge's collapse. This is a stark reminder of the psychosis-induced erosion of trust for government and media, and the perverse online incentive structures that reward the dissemination of misinformation.

THE BIG STORIES. Deceptive symbolism of rebirth, purification, and renewal aside, March 2024 ebbs into a future past as 2.2 billion people now lack access to safely managed drinking water, and about half of the Earth's population continues to experience intermittent severe water scarcity. As global temperatures increase, largely due to the burning of fossil fuels, those numbers are expected to worsen, as higher temperatures will also bring more frequent and intense extreme weather events, including drought. According to a United Nations report,

"Four out of five people lacking at least basic drinking water services lived in rural areas. The situation with respect to safely managed sanitation remains dire, with 3.5 billion people lacking access to such services. Cities and municipalities have been unable to keep up with the accelerating growth of their urban populations."

The U.N. report makes clear that the relationship between conflict and basic human needs is complex, but nonetheless linked. What it boils down to, they signify, is that if the world does not rapidly work to address dwindling water resources, global issues regarding wars, agriculture, migration, and other aspects that allow humanity to prosper, will only intensify.

Summing up the major and potentially devastating issues facing the world, Ian Bremmer, political scientist, author, Time magazine editor, and geopolitics instructor at Columbia University, reminds us that:

- While America's military and economy remain exceptionally strong, the U.S. political system is more dysfunctional than any other advanced industrial democracy. He expects the problem to worsen.

- The fighting in Gaza will expand, with several pathways for escalation into a broader regional war. Some could draw the U.S. and Iran more directly into the fighting. The conflict will pose risks to the global economy, widen geopolitical and political divisions, and stoke global extremism. The straightest path to escalation would be a decision by either Israel or Hezbollah to attack the other.

- Russia's invasion of Ukraine remains an historic failure. NATO is strengthened by new members Finland and Sweden. The European Union has opened a membership process for Ukraine, Russia has faced 11 rounds of sanctions — none very effective — with more on the way. But Ukraine will be de facto partitioned this year, and Russia now has the battlefield initiative and a material advantage. If Ukraine doesn't solve its manpower problems, increase weapons production, and set a realistic military strategy soon, its territorial losses could prove permanent.

- Technology will outstrip AI governance as regulatory efforts falter, tech companies remain largely unconstrained, and far more powerful AI models and tools spread beyond the control of governments.

- Russia, North Korea, and Iran will boost one another's capabilities and act in increasingly coordinated and disruptive ways on the global stage. Meanwhile, even Washington's friends—the leaders of Ukraine, Israel and (potentially) Taiwan—will pull the U.S. into confrontations it wants to avoid.

- This will be another turbulent period for U.S.-China relations, particularly over Taiwan and tech competition, but domestic preoccupations have persuaded Presidents Joe Biden and Xi Jinping that better-managed relations serve both sides.

- The global inflation shock that began in 2021 will continue to exert an economic and political drag in 2024. High interest rates caused by stubborn inflation will slow growth around the world, and governments will have little scope to stimulate growth or respond to shocks, heightening risk of financial stress, social unrest, and political instability.

- After a four-year absence, a powerful El Nino climate pattern will peak in the first half of this year, bringing extreme weather events that trigger food insecurity, increase water stress, disrupt logistics, spread disease, and foment migration and political instability, particularly in countries already weakened by the pandemic and the energy and food prices shocks created by the Ukraine war.

APRIL

"It was a bright cold day in April, and the clocks were striking thirteen." In George Orwell's 1984, the clocks striking thirteen signals a subtle and unsettling change to our own familiar world, previewing a nightmare vision of a future that mirrors the past and undermines the present: The pervasive menace of a military regime, a totalitarian society in which the one-party state can change the number of hours in the day or the way time itself is organized, regulated. We have no control over time. But changing the system by which time is managed is something that tyrants can do, as they control and manipulate us, to give the illusion that they are controlling time as well.

NO LIFE HERE. Israeli forces on Monday, April 1, pulled out of Gaza's largest hospital complex after an intensive two-week military operation, leaving behind charred buildings and bodies strewn at the sprawling complex. Israel said it had battled Palestinian militants hiding inside Gaza City's Al-Shifa Hospital, killed at least 200 enemy fighters, and recovered large stockpiles of weapons, explosives, and cash. Dozens of bodies, some of them decomposed, were recovered from in and around the medical complex. The hospital is said to be completely out of service. A doctor told Agence France-Presse (AFP) more than 20 new bodies had been recovered, some crushed by withdrawing vehicles. Witnesses report a swath of death and destruction at the medical complex, where a large number of displaced Palestinians were sheltering.

The Israeli army announced that 600 of its soldiers had been killed since October 7, 2023. At least 256 soldiers were killed in the Gaza Strip since 27 October, when the retaliatory ground military operation began. Others were killed in the occupied West Bank, or on the border with Lebanon, where there has been an almost daily exchange of fire since 7 October. In addition, more than 1,500 soldiers were wounded in the Palestinian territory since the beginning of the ground operation.

AID WORKERS TARGETED. Outrage continues to spread around the world following Israeli air strikes that killed seven aid workers from the World Central Kitchen (WCK) charity, as the country faces increased scrutiny over its conduct in the war on Gaza. WCK, one of two NGOs spearheading efforts to distribute aid brought by boat, said a *"targeted Israeli strike"* killed Australian, British, Palestinian, Polish and US-Canadian staff. Israeli Prime Minister Netanyahu issued an ambiguous if not callous apology, calling the deaths "an unfortunate wartime accident." The incident has once again raised serious questions about the IDF's opaque and highly permissive rules of engagement, whether those rules are enforced, and how willing it is to investigate breaches. According to a report in the Israeli daily Haaretz, the IDF knew that the vehicles belonged to World Central Kitchen. They targeted them "believing that an armed individual was among the occupants."

The Israeli military's bombing campaign in Gaza used a previously undisclosed AI-powered database that at one stage identified 37,000 potential targets based on their apparent links to Hamas, according to intelligence sources involved in the war. In addition to talking about their use of the AI system, called Lavender, intelligence sources claim that Israeli military officials permitted large numbers of Palestinian civilians to be killed, particularly during the early weeks and months of the conflict. Children account for more than one in three of the more than 32,000 people killed in Israel's months-long assault on Gaza, according to the Palestinian health ministry. Tens of thousands more young people have suffered severe injuries, including amputations.

∽

President Joe Biden told Israeli Prime Minister Netanyahu that the overall humanitarian situation in Gaza is unacceptable and warned Israel to take steps to address the crisis or face consequences, a stark statement from Israel's staunchest ally. The conversation was the two leaders' first phone call since an Israeli strike killed seven aid workers from the World Central Kitchen. That incident has sent off furor inside the White House and Biden has been described as reaching a new level of frustration with Israel's campaign in Gaza. The White House said in a statement issued shortly after the call:

"President Biden emphasized that the strikes on humanitarian workers and the overall humanitarian situation are unacceptable. He made clear that U.S. policy with respect to Gaza will be determined by our assessment of Israel's immediate action on these steps."

Secretary of State Antony Blinken said in Brussels that if the U.S. does not see changes in Israel's policies to protect civilians in Gaza, *"there'll be changes in our own policy."*

Whereupon the IDF dismissed a colonel and a major and conceded to have acted negligently and in violation of accepted rules of engagement.

TREMORS RATTLE TAIWAN. A 7.4 earthquake, the strongest in a quarter of a century, shook Taiwan, causing at least nine deaths and more than 1,000 injuries. Some 30 buildings collapsed. Tremors were also felt in Hong Kong and as far away as China's coastal provinces, some 350 kilometers from the epicenter. redux

SETTLERS RUN AMOK. Hundreds of armed Israeli settlers stormed a village in the occupied West Bank on Friday, setting fire to several homes and cars in one of the largest attacks by settlers this year, according to Palestinian officials. At least one Palestinian man was killed by gunfire. About 25 others were also injured in the rampage, according to the Palestinian Ministry of Health in Ramallah, the scale of which has not been seen since hundreds of settlers stormed through two villages in separate incidents last year.

Israeli security forces had informed Palestinian officials that the settlers were looking for an Israeli teenager who had gone missing earlier in the day and was later found dead. Between 1,000 and 1,200 settlers surrounded the village, and around 500 stormed it, blocking all the roads in the area. The settlers attacked the village, raided homes, and fired guns at residents. Videos obtained by CNN show parts of the village burning, with smoke billowing over several buildings and settlers lobbing rocks. Houses and cars are seen completely burned up, with sounds of gunfire and clashes heard in the background.

IRAN RESPONDS. On the night of Saturday, April 13, to Sunday, April 14, Iran launched 300 drones and missiles from its territory toward Israel. Tehran's attack was unprecedented since the creation of the Israeli state in 1948. For several hours, the skies over Jerusalem, the Golan Heights and the southern Negev were streaked with light trails left by interceptor missiles fired by the Iron Dome and some of Israel's allies.

The offensive was carried out in response to an airstrike on the Iranian consulate in Damascus, Syria, on April 1. Sixteen people were killed in the attack, including two generals of the Revolutionary Guards, the Iranian regime's ideological army. The following day, Iran's supreme leader, Ayatollah Ali Khamenei, pledged that Israel would be "punished." At this writing the incident is being considered as a major escalation in a conflict that is likely to broaden.

❧

For once, a military assault's magnitude was not measured by its outcome. The multidimensional act of aggression Iran launched against Israel, on the night of Saturday, April 13, did not cause major damage, loss of life, territorial annexation, or significant destabilization of Israel's defense system. Quite the contrary. Virtually all the drones were tracked from the moment they were launched and destroyed, as were the ballistic and cruise missiles fired in the second salvo. The operation had been predicted and anticipated for days, both by the Israeli security establishment and its primary protector, the U.S.

Tehran considers itself "avenged." This is a way of

curbing its appetite for war in a tactical game of "chicken" with Washington. It should never be forgotten that Iran is heir to an old, highly sophisticated empire, which has practiced power relations for thousands of years. Its spectacular attack is a model of sophistication, which allows Tehran to create a climate of tension, but without raising the stakes too high. First of all, it is a question of dosage, with these 300 drones and missiles which, given the distance between Iran and Israel—more than 1,600 km—took several hours to reach their potential targets. Secondly, the choice of precisely these targets: minor military installations, as large cities have been carefully avoided. Hezbollah is content to launch a few rockets, and the Yemeni Houthis to board a cargo ship belonging to an Israeli billionaire.

The Iranian communiqué that closes this sequence is a small masterpiece: "Iran considers itself avenged," which means that "we will stop there." Obviously, if Israel retaliates, Iran would be ready for battle, but it does not want it. The desire for war is thus voluntarily restrained. Having said that one should not underestimate Iran's desire to show Israel that it too has become a major military power in the region.

TIT FOR TAT. Early on Friday, April 19, Israel retaliated to the drone and missile attack launched by Iran against its territory six days earlier. Tehran, however, sought to minimize the scale of its response, the nature and details of which remained uncertain in the morning. Explosions were reported near the central city of Isfahan, home to several military sites, including nuclear and ballistic. As it stands, and without prejudging the lethality of the attack, it appears that Israel has chosen a relatively discreet response, leaving Tehran the option of not retaliating. Stay tuned.

A top Hamas political official told The Associated Press that the Islamic militant group is willing to agree to a truce of five years or more with Israel and that it would lay down its weapons and convert into a political party if an independent Palestinian state is established along the pre-1967 borders. If legitimate, the suggestion that Hamas would disarm appears to be a significant concession by a militant group officially committed to Israel's destruction. But it's unlikely Israel would consider such a scenario. It has vowed to crush Hamas following the deadly October 7, 2023, attacks that triggered the war, and the current leadership, like its predecessors, is adamantly opposed to the creation of a Palestinian state on lands Israel captured in the 1967 Mideast war.

Seventeen Israeli diplomats, eminent academics and major political figures have since declared that recognition of a Palestinian state is a matter of principle and historical justice. It is also a way of giving a chance to a return to calm in this war-torn region. Such a significant diplomatic effort would remove the ambiguity that has plagued the entire "peace process" since its inception, put diplomacy back on track, and force the parties to the conflict, as well as key international actors, to assume their responsibility:

> *"We call on Member States of the European Union, the United Kingdom, and other States to take this important step towards a two-State solution. This war must not become yet another chapter in the long history of violence*

between Israelis and Palestinians. There is no better way to restore confidence in diplomacy than to recognize, now, the State of *Palestine."*

Let's see what happens. I'm not holding my breath.

"GREED (FOR LACK OF A BETTER WORD) IS GOOD." Tyson Foods, a Fortune 100 company and the world's second largest meat producer, dumped millions of pounds of toxic pollutants directly into American rivers and lakes over the last five years, threatening critical ecosystems, endangering wildlife and human health, a new investigation reveals. Nitrogen, phosphorus, chloride, oil and cyanide were among the 371 million pounds of pollutants released into waterways by just 41 Tyson slaughterhouses and mega processing plants between 2018 and 2022.

The water pollution from Tyson was spread across 17 states but about half the contaminants were dumped into streams, rivers, lakes and wetlands in Nebraska, Illinois and Missouri. According to research by the Union of Concerned Scientists (UCS), the contaminants were dispersed in 87 billion gallons of wastewater—which also contains blood, bacteria and animal feces—and released directly into streams, rivers, lakes and wetlands relied on for drinking water, fishing and recreation. The UCS analysis, shared exclusively with the Guardian, is based on the most recent publicly available water pollution data Tyson is required to report under current regulations. The wastewater was enough to fill about 132,000 Olympic-size pools.

JEW-HATRED ON DISPLAY. Police officers and

university administrators continue to clash with pro-Palestinian protesters on a growing number of college campuses across the country in recent days, arresting students, removing encampments and threatening academic consequences. The fresh wave of student activism against the war in Gaza was sparked by the arrest of at least 108 protesters at Columbia University, after administrators appeared before Congress and promised a crackdown. Since then, police interventions on 30 campuses, including in some of America's largest cities, have led to more than 1,200 arrests. None of the protesters was willing to discuss the massacre by Hamas infiltrators of 1,200 Israelis on October 7, 2023.

PLASTICMAN. Plastics producers have known for more than 30 years that recycling is not a profit-making or technically viable waste management solution. Plastic waste can take from 20 to 500 years to decompose and even then it never disappears; it just gets smaller and smaller until it is absorbed and becomes embedded in a wide range of living creatures, including the seafood we eat. More recently, microplastics have been found inside the human body: lungs, blood, feces and breast milk. We are literally becoming plasticized. Microplastics have been detected in human testicles, with researchers saying the discovery might be linked to declining sperm counts in men. Sperm counts in men have been falling for decades, with chemical pollution such as pesticides implicated by many studies.

That has not stopped the industry from promoting it, according to a report published by the Center for Climate Integrity, a fossil-fuel accountability advocacy group which alleges that big oil and gas companies learned decades ago that burning fossil fuels would lead to "catastrophic" climate change. Instead of doing the right thing, they masterminded a decades-long, multimillion dollar climate denial, disinformation, and deception campaign to delay climate action and protect their profits.

Made from oil and gas, plastic is notoriously difficult to recycle. Doing so requires meticulous sorting, since most of the thousands of chemically distinct varieties of plastic cannot be recycled together. The industry has known for decades about these existential challenges, but obscured that information in its marketing campaigns, the report concluded. The research draws on previous investigations as well as newly revealed internal documents illustrating the extent of this decades-long campaign of obfuscation. It's the same greed, mendacity, and brazen willingness to undermine scientific evidence and sacrifice humans in the pursuit of profits that led cigarette manufacturers, 70 years ago, to conceal evidence that smoking is harmful and potentially deadly. It's the American Way.

MAY

The month of May holds significant historical importance in various cultures and societies around the world. One of the most well-known historical events associated with May is the celebration of May Day, also known as International Workers' Day, which commemorates the Haymarket massacre in Chicago in 1886. The U.S. enters into several treaties each year on a range of international issues, but it consistently fails to sign or ratify treaties the rest of the world supports. It has failed to ratify treaties that tackle biodiversity and greenhouse gas emissions, protect the rights of children and women, and govern international waters. For a country frequently looked to as a global leader, the U.S. has consistently failed to step up in international partnerships. In fact, the U. S. has one of the worst records of any country in ratifying human rights and environmental treaties. It shuns treaties that appear to subordinate its governing authority to that of an international body like the United Nations and the International Court of Justice. To date, 196 nations have signed the United Nations Convention on the Rights of the Child, an international human rights treaty which sets out the civil, political, economic, social, health and cultural rights of children. The U.S. signed the covenant but refuses to ratify it.

JOURNALISM AT THE CROSSROADS. More than 70% of environmental journalists have been attacked for their work since 2009, according to a UNESCO report, which warns of rising threats against those covering the climate crisis. At least 749 environmental journalists have faced violence and intimidation in the last 15 years, the UN body found. It said that 44 reporters were murdered between 2009 and 2023 but that resulted in just five convictions. Environmental journalism has become an increasingly perilous field. The often-remote and isolated nature of the work, and the subject matter reported on, including fossil fuel companies, mining firms, land grabbing and deforestation, contributed to the danger. Physical violence—including assaults, arbitrary detention, murder attempts and abductions—were the most common form of attack and have since risen to alarming levels.

According to the Committee to Protect Journalists, as of May 3, 97 journalists and media workers were confirmed dead: 92 Palestinian, 2 Israeli, and 3 Lebanese. More than 16 journalists were reported injured; four were reported missing, and 25 were reported jailed by Israel. Israel bans foreign media outlets from entering Gaza, forcing them to report from Tel Aviv, Jerusalem or southern Israel. On Israeli territory, they must comply with the rules and censorship of the Israeli Military Censor, which is part of the Israeli army and requires media materials be submitted for its review prior to publication or broadcasting. Israel's parliament also passed a law allowing its government to ban foreign news networks perceived to be posing a threat to national security. Israel's Prime Minister Benjamin Netanyahu has vowed to shut down Al Jazeera. Since the start of the war, the Qatari-based network, which has offices in Israel, has produced critical, on-the-ground coverage of Israel's military operations and their humanitarian impact on the embattled Gazan enclave. The Foreign Press Association in Israel described the Netanyahu's decision as *"a dark day for democracy"* and *"a cause for concern for all supporters of a free press."*

STUDENTS STORM UNIVERSITIES. And lo and behold, college campuses across the U.S. erupted with disorderly, often violent pro-Palestinian protests that neither school administrators nor law enforcement have been able to defuse. Tensions on U.S. college campuses have risen since October 7 raid, when Hamas militants slaughtered about 1,200 people and took more than 200 hostages. Israel's retaliatory assault on Gaza has since killed more than 37,000 people, according to its health ministry. Antisemitic acts have surged across America, lending credence to the widespread suspicion that the protests were infiltrated and in some cases led by members of some of the 1,000 neo-Nazi groups that proliferate across America.

In addition to New York's Columbia University, pro-Palestinian encampments have been set up at the Massachusetts Institute of Technology, Emerson College, the University of Texas at Austin, the University of Michigan and the University of California, Berkeley. Police arrested nearly 100 protesters at the University of Southern California after a dispersal order. Yale University police arrested at least 45 protesters and charged them with criminal trespassing after they refused orders to leave. Harvard University closed Harvard Yard and officials at the school suspended a pro-Palestinian student organization for allegedly violating school policies. Meanwhile, nine people were arrested at the University of Minnesota's Twin Cities campus after they formed an encampment that went against school policy. Students, faculty and staff at the University of New Mexico peacefully protested Monday in support of Gaza. More than 100 people were arrested at Emerson College in Boston.

I polled a number of openly anti-Zionists of my acquaintance, offering to join the rallies to mourn the death of thousands of innocent Palestinian civilians killed by the IDF in Gaza if they conceded that Hamas had committed atrocities on October 7, 2023. They declined. So much for parity.

Antisemitism is not being "imported" into the U.S., as

some misinformed or malevolent voices claim. It has always existed. The first governmental incident of anti-Jewish action came during the American Civil War, when General Ulysses S. Grant issued Order No. 11 to expel Jews from Tennessee, Kentucky and Mississippi then under his control. The order was quickly rescinded by President Lincoln, but not before a large number of Jews were forcibly removed from their homes.

From the 1870s to the 1940s, Jews were routinely discriminated against and barred from working in some fields of employment, barred from owning or residing certain properties, not accepted as members by elite social clubs, barred from resort areas and limited by quotas in enrolling in elite colleges. Antisemitism reached its peak with the rise of the second Ku Klux Klan in the 1920s, antisemitic publications by Henry Ford, and incendiary radio speeches by neo-Nazi Father Coughlin in the late 1930s. The U.S. knew that Jews were being massacred in Hitler's slaughterhouses. It didn't react. Antisemitism has since undergone a resurgence. I continue to argue that Kristallnacht can happen again, right here in Amerika the Beautiful.

THE EVER-ELUSIVE CEASEFIRE. Meanwhile, several heads of state warned that Israel would be committing a war crime under international law if it seeks to forcibly displace 100,000 Palestinian refugees as part of a military effort to drive the remaining Hamas battalions out of Gaza.

The Israeli army entered Rafah on May 7 after carrying out intense shelling in the southern Gaza Strip city. The Civil Defense in the Gaza Strip reported "many deaths" overnight. And the Kuwaiti hospital, located in Rafah, said it had received "11 dead" and "dozens wounded" in the strikes. For its part, the Israel Defense Forces claim that the rockets fired during the day towards the Jewish state were fired from Rafah. After its operations in Gaza City, then Khan Younis, Israel has been threatening for weeks to push its ground offensive as far as Rafah, considered the last stronghold of Hamas but where 1.2 million Palestinians are still crammed, most of them displaced by the fighting.

ABOLUTE POWER CORRUPTS ABSOLUTELY. Vladimir Putin began his fifth term on Tuesday, May 7, as Russian leader at a glittering Kremlin inauguration, setting out on another six years in office after destroying his political opponents, launching a devastating war in Ukraine and concentrating all power in his hands. Already in office for nearly a quarter-century and the longest-serving Kremlin leader since Josef Stalin, Putin's new term doesn't expire until 2030, when he will be eligible to run again.

Shortly before the inauguration, Russian opposition figure Yulia Navalnaya, widow of assassinated opposition leader, Alexei Navalny, declared:

"Our country is being led by a liar, a thief and a murderer. But this will definitely come to an end."

Adding that Putin's latest term was marked by a war in Ukraine that is bloody and senseless and political repression in Russia, Navalnaya, who lives in exile, vowed to continue her husband's fight.

❧

Need I continue? The history of the world is a repetition, the habituated replication of a failed but relentlessly resurrected past. In his *Myth of Sisyphus*, French author/philosopher Albert Camus (1913-1960) likened the absurdity of man's existence to the ordeal of Sisyphus, a figure of Greek legend who was condemned to repeat for eternity the same meaningless task of pushing a boulder up a mountain, only to see it roll down again just as it nears the top. He pithily summed up humanity's existential dilemma by remarking that men are woefully unaware of the tremendous energy they must exert just to be normal—"normality" being the antithesis of the individualism essential in resisting, defying, agitating against rote conformity. He urged:

> *"The only way to deal with an unfree world is to become so absolutely free that your very existence is an act of rebellion."*

In my world (and in Einstein's—who coined the saying),

> *"Doing the same thing repeatedly, while expecting a different outcome is the definition of insanity."*

Einstein was being kind. He surely meant cretinism, not lunacy. In reasonably free societies, no one is condemned or fated to do the same thing over and over. We have choices. The fact that we ignore them is proof that the obvious escapes us, that we have learned nothing from history, that we spurn it in hopes of exorcising its noxious lessons. We are hopeless philistines.

As we boldly plant the seeds of our demise, confident that cretinism, a contagious malady among humans, will add many more examples of its power to subvert reason and the truth, I am at this point suspending this senseless and unending inventory of bad news. I shall now move on from postmortem to etiology [causation].

∽∾

As I take leave of this depressing recitation and bid the month of May farewell, I am delighted to learn that Julian Assange who, after losing his latest appeal against extradition to the U.S., where he faces fake charges under the Espionage Act of leaking military secrets, was finally granted leave to mount a fresh appeal. He will be able to challenge questionable assurances from American officials on how a trial would be conducted. The ailing 52-year-old Assange is wanted by U.S. authorities on 18 criminal counts after WikiLeaks, the organization he founded, published thousands of damning classified documents and diplomatic cables in 2010 and 2011. Assange did not commit a prosecutable crime. So, the U.S. is conspiring to snare him on trumped-up charges of ... sexual misconduct ... in Sweden. Ah, Big Brother.

Wikileaks epitomizes investigative journalism at its finest. Everyone is fair game: politicians, corporations, and private interests dedicated to the enrichment of a small clique through deception, surveillance, war, economic colonialism, and exploitation, extraordinary rendition, and assassination. Assange has an ironclad First Amendment argument. He is no different than a newspaper editor who receives classified documents and publishes them. Maybe fewer secrets, greater transparency, and cordial dialogue can do more to cement good relations between people than backroom intrigues, covert operations, and the lies that must be told to conceal or justify them. Alas, if we let him, Big Brother has the power to turn virtue into sin, integrity into crime. Which is why the world needs the likes of Julian Assange to shake things up.

Nor can I contain my relief upon learning of the death of Iranian President Ebrahim Raisi in a helicopter crash after hours of denials and contradictory information from the Iranian media. Raisi, a ruthless prosecutor linked to thousands of mass executions, rose through the theocratic ranks to become Iran's president. Accused of being one of the four judges who oversaw the slaughter of thousands of political prisoners, he was routinely referred to as the "Butcher of Tehran." According to Human Rights Watch, Iran has never acknowledged what has been described as the massacre of an estimated 2,800 to 5,000 people.

Last, while no one is facing imminent arrest, I hail the symbolic significance of the decision by International Criminal Court to prosecute Israeli Prime Minister Benjamin Netanyahu, his defense minister, and three Hamas leaders for war crimes and crimes against humanity in the Gaza Strip and Israel.

JUNE
JULY
AUGUST
SEPTEMBER
OCTOBER
NOVEMBER
DECEMBER
?

THE BONEYARD OF ABSURDITY
The "good old days"

The world as we knew it ended several times before our common era and survivors, after a brief period of fake repentance, proceeded to ravage the world once again until the first signs of yet another impending day of reckoning loomed large on humanity's horizon.

Will our reincarnated doppelgangers of, say, the 31st century, be pondering the next *Götterdämmerung*? The ultimate end, we are told, will come when the Sun dies in a final blaze of glory. As it expands, Earth will get so hot that the oceans will boil and evaporate. The planet, now a burning husk, will be pulled to the sun's surface and vaporize. By then, the world will have spawned a few prodigies and a huge number of imbeciles and villains. All attempts to establish sustainable extraterrestrial human settlements having failed, those of us who did not succumb to greed, hatred, or terminal stupidity, will marvel at the grand spectacle of one last twilight while the faithful seek help from an entity that has remained consistently blind, deaf, mute, and indifferent to human suffering. The past is prelude. Isaiah commands:

> *"Learn to do right; seek justice. Defend the oppressed. Take up the cause of the fatherless; plead the case of the widow."*

Luke affirms:

> *"Whoever yearns for freedom, justice, and peace may rise again and raise his head, for in Christ liberation is drawing near."*

The Quran teaches:

"Allah forgives all sins. Verily, he is most merciful."

And the Code of Hammurabi, which precedes them all, vows to,

"bring about the rule of righteousness in the land, so that the strong should not harm the weak."

Somehow, these ancient pleas turned out to be hollow, cruel hoaxes. Moses' ten, simple directives are habitually and maliciously violated. Jesus—the "Savior," an unsuccessful demagogue—saved nothing. Allah forgives only those who surrender to him. Convulsing under rising waves of ignorance, hatred, and inanity, racked by spasms of violence, planet Earth still awaits salvation—from itself. In defiance of half-hearted warnings by the *"First World,"* crippled by poverty, ethnic strife, and the clash of cultures, sundered by shifting loyalties, withering *"developing"* nations indulge in or succumb to genocide. Yearning for social justice, economic parity, and independence from their puppet masters, lurching from restlessness to inertia, succeeding generations teeter on the brink of civil war, or have succumbed to it. All around the world, earthlings struggle to preserve increasingly shrinking fragments of their ancestral domains. Global warming is putting polar regions on thin ice, threatening to inundate coastal areas and engulf dozens of islands. Warning that artificial intelligence could one day wipe out the human race, the late physicist Stephen Hawking (1942-2018) wrote:

"One can imagine AI outsmarting financial markets, out-inventing human researchers, out-manipulating human

leaders, out-developing weapons we cannot even understand. Whereas the short-term effect of AI depends on who controls it, the long-term impact depends on whether it can be controlled at all."

Embroiled in unwinnable wars it knows how to start but doesn't really care to end, the U.S. clings to the two-party system, both factions the flip-sides of the same tarnished coin, both indistinguishable one from the other except for the sparring partisanships they engender and the antipathies they inspire, both tied to corporate wealth, both committed to blocking meaningful reforms in the name of Wall Street-controlled crony capitalism, both involved in larceny against the poor. Justice has been subverted by the aggregate interests of the dominant power base.

The chasm between the haves and have-nots continues to widen. The Catholic Church, the richest empire on earth and the self-appointed moral arbiter to millions, is embroiled in sordid scandals. Living in Babylonian splendor, basking in the idolatrous reverence of the flock, *princes* of the Church sneer at mankind's earthly struggles. Intoxicated by the apocalyptic rants found in Revelation, Evangelical Christians yearn for an all-consuming Armageddon during which the Jews will be wiped out. The crucifixion of Jesus of Nazareth—if he ever existed—is a fitting metaphor for man's inhumanity to man. Its continued commemoration (and pretext for the commission of more atrocities) in the aftermath of the Crusades, the *Holy* Inquisition, the Armenian and Jewish holocausts, the wars of conquest, liberation, "democratiz-ation," and retribution, reminds us that salvation, like justice, human rights, compassion, ethics, and love, remains a distant vision, not a serious objective. Nothing has changed. From the time of Jesus to the present, the world has been lacerated by violence and degraded by injustice. Christians have shed more blood in Christ's name than all other people. In the 13th century, Genghis Khan could not recognize the world that Attila had conquered five centuries earlier. In the 1950s, my grandmother, a child of the *Gay 90s*, could not recognize the genteel milieu in which she had been raised. This disembodiment from the dreary realities of the past is what drives some of us to look in the rear-view mirror with rose-tinted glasses while scuttling any prospect of a better tomorrow. We are the same sanguinary creatures we always were. Only some of the pretense has rubbed off. Educated, worldly, my grandmother was astute enough to admit that the differences are merely cosmetic:

"People were as lustful and debauched and hypocritical and corruptible and greedy and habituated to war when I was a young girl as they are now. They just dressed differently, put on prudish airs, and talked about the good old days."

❧

In the past three decades, ongoing conflicts around the globe have claimed more than five million lives. People continue to die in Afghanistan and Colombia, Gaza and Israel, Iraq and Libya, Somalia and Sudan. Insurgencies and sectarian rivalries in Southeast Asia, sub-Saharan Africa, and Latin America are claiming many more lives. Displaced by war, poverty, hunger, and persecution, some 50 million people have been forced to flee and seek refuge in countries that are hard-pressed to absorb them, shelter them, nourish them. The ongoing exodus is feeding resentment, xenophobia, racism, and violence

History is written then retouched, tweaked. One man's truth is another man's conspiracy theory. The allure of history rests not only on the events it records but in the chronicler's subjective interpretations and inferences. Without these adornments, the annals of man would consist of little more than a terse compendium of facts and dates. Whereas some social scientists tend to interpret history as an evolution from savagery to emotional maturity and intellectual refinement, reality is far less comforting. In the aggregate, human society seesaws wildly between states of stagnancy, feverish creativity, restlessness, madness, and turmoil. While these oscillations can be blamed on the cretins, killers, and kleptocrats we elect (or surrender to) they are hastened, prolonged and fossilized by the appalling lethargy or recklessness of the masses. Voltaire wrote:

"History is a lie commonly agreed upon."

Yes, victors write history to justify and exalt conquest; losers to mitigate defeat. Neither side will concede the other's account. The Turks deny exterminating a million or more Armenians. Followers of the Bushido code of honor, some Japanese worship war criminals. Seventy years after the fall of the Third Reich, some Germans insist the only mistake Germany made ... was to lose the war. These horrors remind us that the worst villainies are committed by those who disremember the past, falsify the facts and dehumanize their rivals.

❧

The axiom that the world's fate is in the hands of bankers and industrialists is never more fittingly demonstrated than in wartime. The lords of capital and the cannon merchants salivate at the prospect—and unfolding—of armed conflicts. Pillaging the national treasury and fleecing taxpayers, they thrive when the first shots ring out. And so, military transports will continue to unload body bags and flag-draped caskets. Posthumous medals will be cast to salute young people who die in illegal, immoral, and unwinnable wars they did not declare or chose to fight. Bugles will play taps and three-rifle volleys will ring out in the grief-filled stillness of a hundred cemeteries.

Burkina Faso. Niger. Mali. Myanmar. Cashmere. Yemen. Syria, Ukraine, Gaza, and the West Bank, to name a few distant locales that experience horrendous levels of violence. In America people kill and get killed for a grudge, the wrong word, a domestic squabble, an employee grievance, road rage, a minor fender-bender, a legal dispute. Mass-shootings are generally the work of deranged individuals but they are abetted by the unregulated availability of firearms. The country is drowning in guns. Yes, some countries experience violence but it is usually triggered by specific internal convulsions or by war. The U.S. is the only country I know that has—since its birth—an entrenched culture of violence. Movies are violent. TV programs are violent. TV commercials are strident and hinting at violence. American sports are violent for violence's stake. What passes for music in this country not only lacks melody and harmony but is ear-splitting and performed by artists who seem possessed by a diabolic energy that is patently violent. The political process is confrontational and violent. The right to bear arms (Second Amendment, enacted in 1791) feeds the willingness, if not the urge to use them. Americans are in love with their guns and, as witnessed by an epidemic of mass shootings and daily homicides, don't hesitate to use them. Everybody is armed. Things are so bad that you have to think twice before getting into a verbal altercation. People are getting shot (and killed) for a trifle—a sidelong glance, an ambiguous gesture, a poor choice of words. Interfere with a driver who insists on going twice the speed limit and he is liable to pull a gun on you. This is happening every day, everywhere in the country. I would argue that America not only has a culture of violence but that it worships violence as a means of self-expression. Road traffic is violent. Aggressive driving is a form of homicidal/suicidal violence. Even women have become contentious, argumentative, overly aggressive. (I suppose having to deal with American males would drive an angel mad…). And I am convinced that soaring racism and ethnic hatreds will fuel more violence.

Sadly, we cannot adjust to being human. We listen to village idiots who tell us that science is a hoax, reason a deception, fact is fake news. We humans are generally stupid, corruptible, wicked, and prone to madness. Venturing into the realm of "possibility" vs. "probability" leads to a philosophical impasse and slippery slope: It suggests that even in the absence of empirical evidence, a theory has a 50/50 chance of being averred true … opening up the theory that *god* exists. Where does faith begin and reason end?

Of course, it makes scientific sense to assume (but again without the slightest proof) that at least one planet in our 93 billion lightyears-wide universe (a figure that cosmologists pulled out of their rectum) is inhabited by rational, honest, kind, and enlightened beings. Maybe.

One could otherwise argue that if the universe is teeming with various life forms, including advanced, "intelligent, civilized" ones, a conscious, result-driven "master plan" is at play, thus suggesting the work of a "principal creator" — (*god*?) — whereas if life is confined to planet Earth … it's a fluke, a coincidence, an accident. an unrepeatable abomination. It is because we don't know one way or the other that our speculations are the product of our optic, fantasy, and perhaps secret longings rather than irrefutable knowledge.

In a tale, as in a revolution, the most difficult part to invent is the ending. Storytellers must not only have a flair for history; they must also own up to it. An ending is not supposed to be a surprise. To envision the kind of ominous climax hinted in this narrative — that creation's payback is disorder, collapse, and extinction — readers must also reflect on the paroxysms of lunacy and violence that lend it credence, that are apt to hasten them. One facet of madness is the willingness to kill, or die, for an idea.

GET OVER IT
An opinion is not a fact & other annoying facts

I hear it uttered, often with censorious annoyance *"I'm entitled to my opinions."* Sure, but an opinion is not a fact. Unless you're Aquinas or Aristotle, Socrates or Sartre, Spinoza, Descartes or Camus, your opinions are likely mundane, borrowed, inflexible, or trivial. Even my polarizing takes on the human condition, valid as they might be, can easily be invalidated by a louder, more menacing voice. We generally adopt those positions that most closely harmonize with the drummed-in beliefs and prejudices of our parents, teachers, "spiritual advisors," and favorite shock-jocks. We cling to them because independent and critical thinking require an enormous capital of intellectual latitude and moral courage, not to mention a gray matter uncontaminated by immovable beliefs. Worse, we shamelessly peddle them while being convinced of our own deductive faculties. The great tragedy is that few of us grasp or care about the lies that opinions often conceal. They are the dungeons in which we lock ourselves by feigning a clear conscience—very often the result of a bad memory. Most of our viewpoints are built on a vast scaffolding of dogmas, doctrines, preconceptions, and chimeras often advanced by someone else. And yet we believe that they are the result of our own ruminations because ignorance reinforced by conceit protects us from what we fear most—the truth. Paradoxically, ignorance makes us happy. I have always suspected that happy people are just too stupid to be unhappy. Or, as Michel de Montaigne (1533-1592), one of the most significant philosophers of the French Renaissance suggested,

> *"That's why ignorance is so strongly recommended to us by religion as the appropriate path to belief and obedience."*

Everybody has opinions. Naïve or wacky, they are easily deconstructed and dismissed. Stubborn or toxic, they blind us, inflate us with arrogance. Taken to the extreme, they drive us mad. Opining from emotion does the truth a disservice. It just makes us feel better about ourselves because, heavens forbid, we should be wrong about anything that comes out unreflexively out of our mouths. And yet, they're the devices with which the truth is often sacrificed. Without them there would be nothing to talk about.

It's not a question of semantics or the ambiguities of personal perception. Clearly, an opinion is universally understood as a view or judgment formed about something, but not necessarily based on fact or empirical knowledge. When we opine, we express a subjunctive feeling, we betray an attitude, we articulate a sentiment, a penchant, not a verity. Whether a statement is a fact or an opinion depends on the validity of the statement. Fact refers to something true or real, which is backed by evidence, observation, verification. On the other hand, an opinion is what we *believe, assume,* or *hope* something to be. A fact is a proven truth, whereas an opinion is a personal view (or a statement of blind faith): *god* created the heavens and the earth is six days and rested on the seventh; Jesus was born by parthenogenesis; Elvis is alive; the Holocaust is a myth; the Moon landing was a fake; the CIA had a hand in JFK's assassination; 9/11 was an inside job perpetrated by the Jews; top Democrats are behind a child sex ring; the Earth is flat: and my all-time favorite, COVID-19 is an attempt at population control. (During the "Holy" Inquisition, Jews were accused of poisoning wells and causing the Black Death). Today they are accused of starting wildfires with "space lasers," a fantasy concocted by ignorant idiots ... and spread by other imbeciles.

At best, opinions impart second-hand views endlessly retold, recast, and misread: the idiosyncratic, hand-me-down, robotic indoctrinations to which we are subject from the youngest age; the lies our parents feed us; the expedient reinterpretations of history; the often-slanted pedagogy of our teachers; the absurd credos and intimidating ultimatums of religion; the partisan reflections of party politics. At worst, cleverly packaged, cunningly marketed, opinions masquerading as fact (or Gospel truth ...) have the power to anesthetize or agitate men, lead them to the kind of mass frenzy and violence to which history has been witness. In short, all opinions are adopted, then often forced on others. They are artificial, self-perpetuating concepts. Born with a blank slate, a child has no opinions. Deprived of a broad view of reality, he/she, like sheep, follows the flock. How often have you heard someone say, "My daddy was a Republican (or Democrat) ... and, ergo, so am I." Such people are not concerned with truth. They're intellectually comatose. They're in fact devoid of opinions. They just wallow in unquestioning self-satisfaction about the views they cling to.

When fact is ignored or contradicted, all that's left is

opinion, inference, speculation. It's difficult if not impossible to concur with or refute an opinion without a solid grasp of the underlying facts. It has been my experience that most people are either too stupid to distinguish between fact and fancy, too lazy to mine for the truth, or too enamored with their precious conclusions. The rest is all speculation. In the absence of fact, humans speculate. The whole human drama is one long, loud, boring conjecture.

∽

I have become fascinated by the debate between Anthropocene anti-humanism, inspired by the revulsion toward man's unceasing assault on nature—humanity is essentially a destroyer—and transhumanism (which glorifies scientific progress and technology, banks on the grim supremacy of artificial intelligence, and insists that man's only path to the future is to create new life forms that in no way resemble Homo sapiens).

I dislike transhumanists. I just don't buy into their fantasy. The end of the human race is in fact a highly positive event as it would give our planet a second chance, an opportunity to recover, restore biodiversity and maybe, who knows, produce a truly intelligent species. I believe it is a colossal error to call humans "intelligent." We are not. We are semi-intelligent or better yet, "quasi-intelligent." Reason plays a very minor part in our decisions. Most people can live all their lives without even thinking once. The chaos mankind has wrought upon itself since Cain murdered Abel is ample proof that opinion, ego, and inflexible beliefs are the enemies of truth.

❦

Fascism is a brand of extreme patriotism typified by hatred, racism, and the messianic affectations of banner-waving halfwits. Valiant when they outnumber their detractors, always itching for a fight, fascists dread the ridicule their slogans and cocky bearing inspire because without the swagger, goth tattoos, insignias, tactical vests, boots, and combat helmets, they are little more than pitiable buffoons.

Nationalism is the catechism of fascism. Charitably defined as a sense of shared consciousness or an exaltation of one's own nation and feelings of cultural superiority, fascism aims to establish an obedient society whose reverence, energies, and labors are unconditionally devoted to the sustenance of the party.

American nationalism has two faces. Libertarians, the high-priests of neoconservatism, some of whom traded white robes and hoods for teabags, believe that they can control the future (as their patron-saint, Ayn Rand, preached) purely on self-interest, laissez-faire, and isolationism. They do not openly endorse violence. They prefer to be seen as visionaries and pragmatists. They are committed neither to democracy nor civil liberties. They simply lack the courage to call themselves fascists. Ordinary fascists don't care how they are perceived. Pretending to be the downtrodden, they assert that *god* and the Constitution give them the right to do what democracy abhors: sedition, secessionism, and the circumvention of legitimate government oversight. They revere dictators and war criminals, and swoon with nostalgia over America's supremacist past. Engaged in a constant assault on democratic norms, they embody the kind of intellectual rigidity, zealotry, ignorance, and psychoses that inspired the storming of the Capitol. Libertarians and ordinary fascists, neocons, and neo-Confederate skinheads all aspire to suppress democratic principles, erudition, culture, and dissent under the leadership of a charismatic führer who will assume quasi-divine status. Although essentially homegrown, U.S. nationalists like to quote Mussolini, Hitler, Goebbels, and other lunatics. Stirred by far-right presidential contenders they work to agitate a furious, forever antagonistic America.

Fascism's most consistent feature is antisemitism. When fascists clamor against capitalism, they always whine against the *"kikes."* Embarked on a spiritual revolution dedicated to the redemption of the white race, they aim to create a new Christian Utopia by purging socialist interlopers. They yearn for a nation cleansed of Jews, whom they accuse of conspiring against freedom-loving Americans. The Southern Poverty Law Center is tracking some 700 right-wing hate groups in the U.S. More than 50 operate in Florida, fascism's new laboratory, including the anti-government terrorist Proud Boys, Oath Keepers, and Stormfront.

The U.S. is now increasingly vulnerable to domestic terror assaults by fascist lone wolves as inflammatory Republican lies are likely to ignite passions ahead of the November 2024 elections. The potential for racially motivated violence has never been greater, as mushrooming far-right terrorism and a string of police-involved incidents have demonstrated. Nothing threatens the future more than willful, villainous indifference toward the past.

⤬

A central argument in *Antigone*, a play by Sophocles (496-405 BC) in which is uttered the famous epigram, *"No one likes the bearer of bad news,"* is the implied right to reject society's infringements, to tally them, expose them, and condemn them.

Journalists and whistleblowers—often one and the same--have one thing in common. They're perceived as arrogant, insensitive, and vexing meddlers. Their disclosures are seldom applauded. Both seek the truth, one in the interest of historicity, the other in the service of justice when history is sacrificed on the altar of special interests. They become indispensable when democracy is trivialized and threatened by mass myopia, lies, unyielding beliefs, and the intellectual hermetism of *barbarians* who, to paraphrase distinguished Spanish philosopher, José Ortega y Gasset (1883-1955),

> *"... harbor a deep hatred of all that is not themselves — hatred being a feeling which leads to the extinction of values."*

Surveying the disconnect between reliable reporting and public perception, Ortega wryly warns that—

> *"The characteristic note of our time is the dire truth that, the mediocre soul, the commonplace mind, knowing itself to be mediocre, has the gall to assert its right to mediocrity, and goes on to impose itself where it can. The present-day writer, when he takes his pen in hand to treat a subject which he has studied deeply, has to bear in mind that the*

average reader, who has never concerned himself with this subject, if he reads at all, does so with the view, not of learning something from the writer, but rather, of pronouncing judgment on him when he is not in agreement with the commonplaces that the said reader carries in his head."

The relentless frustration journalists and whistleblowers endure is not the carping of know-nothing diehards who enjoy hearing themselves orate, but the cowardice and perfidy of those who choose silence out of fear, expediency, and ideological sloth, and the incessant battologizing of people in high places who engage in crypto-fascist prattle crafted to portray incorruptible and outspoken members of the press as gadflies, mudslingers, busybodies, *"purveyors of fake news,"* agents of social discontent, blabbermouths who threaten the *"established order,"* and *"enemies of the people."*

Being a muckraker and a curmudgeon, as I have often been labelled, has its own notable rewards. Unlike myth-peddlers and bearers of glad tidings, muckrakers are heard — hated, but heard. Which is why journalism has become a perilous occupation. For years, I thought that one way of erring on the side of justice was to side unerringly with the victims of injustice — the vanquished, the persecuted, the forgotten. Behind prison walls. At mass graves and hurriedly dug sepulchers. Wherever voices of dissent and cries for freedom are being hushed. Amid the anonymous bones scattered about the steaming earth. Political chicanery, xenophobia, racism, pogroms, *"extraordinary rendition"* [kidnapping], *"enhanced interrogation"* [torture] war, genocide, ethnic cleansing —

they all become a blur in an unceasing tempest of human agony.

Telling inconvenient truths is risky business. I know. I've been in the trenches as tracer bullets whizzed over my head. I was grazed once or twice. Had my reflexes failed me when I spoke of political corruption, police brutality, and military crimes, I might not be vexing you today.

Much still begs to be unearthed, revealed, and dissected. Words survive in the two-dimensional realm of a book or opinion page, but they fail to generate lasting change. Instead, they leave a wasteland of rhetoric that does nothing to alter human nature, chill passions, crush hatred. Some horrors are simply too shocking for words. Is truth-telling worth the wall of odium and discord it raises? I struggle with that question with every stroke of the pen. I will keep on writing. But as I do, I can envisage the day when my pen runs dry in a river of ink whose course was diverted by some unhinged fanatic in high office. Mark my words. That day is near. The floodgates of lunacy are now wide open.

THE FLOODGATES OF LUNACY
The unlearned lessons

Now, any suggestion that my expositions betray repressed political ambitions, that they conceal some veiled inclination to run for office is as comical as it is baseless. I never had the urge to join this, the ugliest cabal of greedy profiteers—politicians—egomaniacs whose sole aims are power, not truth, influence, not justice, self-enrichment, not egalitarianism, and whose only ethos is to put themselves in a position to do major thieving. I can affirm without fear of contradiction that my spartan wartime upbringing, vagrant, restless way of life, utter lack of self-importance, lifelong disdain for money, congenital inability to earn it and, once earned, to hold on to it or make it grow, as well as an abhorrence of politics are not the attributes of a successful thief ... or politician. The radical changes that my critiques imply (I itemize them below) make me patently unelectable, not to mention a prime target for assassination. But since this is a work of liberating self-revelation as much as a condemnation of human folly, it should be no surprise, viewed from a strictly personal perspective, the only one that offers me the luxury of catharsis, that I am not a fan of America. The near-extermination of indigenous peoples as slavery fueled its economy; the impudent commandeering of Hawaii, the Philippines, Cuba, and Puerto Rico; the environmental harm and health risks caused by dozens of nuclear tests carried out in the 1940s and '50s; the deliberate slaughter of at least 200,000 Japanese in Hiroshima and Nagasaki; the quasi-erotic obsession that Americans have with their guns, not to mention their eagerness to use them; the violent sports to which they are addicted; the hero worship—thespians and crooners, most of dubious talent, fictional celluloid Übermenschen, comely people of both genders; raucous divas who strut on stage half-naked and whose celebrity rests entirely on their semi-exposed udders and the amplitude of their gyrating buttocks; and testosterone-bursting "athletes," most of them unremarkable human beings who but for their height, brawn, or dexterity with some implement (a ball, club, stick or pair of boxing gloves)—all of whom would be living in obscurity or standing at the far end of a long unemployment line instead of being lionized and earning obscenely high wages ... all of which led me to view America as a nation of hot-headed brawlers and crude idolaters. An incurable European and supporter of parliamentary democracy, a system where the government is accountable to the legislature and in which the head of government comes to power by gaining the confidence of an elected legislature, I find America's presidentialism archaic and structurally undemocratic. Such unitary system has the potential for gridlock, it inhibits the change in leadership that a crisis might call for, and can give way to a dictatorship. The reforms I would propose—inconceivable in present day America, and for which, once aired, I would undoubtedly be drawn and quartered, are itemized below.

The "Founding Fathers." We should be careful not to rhapsodize America's architects. The *"liberty and justice for all"* they advocated were self-directed and narrow, not universal. They were all landowners wed to capitalist values, including the "right to property" which, by its very essence, excludes those who own nothing (the slaves) and those from whom (Native Nations) that property (America) was stolen. Forty-one of the 56 signers of the Declaration of Independence owned slaves. One of Jefferson's policies was to push *"Indians"* to the other side of the Mississippi River and to kill those who resisted. His Constitution is a telling document that should be understood by what it does not say. When the "Founding Fathers" wrote ... *"to establish Justice, ensure domestic Tranquility, provide for the common defense, promote the general Welfare, and secure the Blessings of Liberty to ourselves and our Posterity,"* they meant for *"us"* — the White Anglo-Saxon Protestant planter aristocracy, the proprietors — not *them*, for the privileged classes, not the low-born landless masses, the slaves, or the aboriginal tribes they dispossessed, displaced, and massacred.

The Constitution. Representative democracy is a form of political redlining. The Electoral College is an archaism, a flawed system, and a disgrace. It violates the core tenet of democracy that all votes count equally. It gives too much power to "swing" states and allows the presidential election to be decided by a handful of states. It is rooted in slavery and racism. Democracy should function on the will of the people, allowing one vote per adult. What's the point of holding an election if a convoluted and devious calculus allows the candidate finishing last to be declared the winner? Remedy: universal suffrage, plebiscites, referenda. One-man one vote. I find bewildering the number of legal loopholes that encourage people to pick and choose the constitutional concepts and mandates they are willing to embrace, and those they fiercely believe they are entitled to disregard.

Political shenanigans. Gerrymandering, a diabolical scheme designed to shift the balance of power along racial or economic lines, should be outlawed. The two-party system — both parties the obverse sides of the same tarnished coin, both at best apathetic to meaningful restructurings and at worst downright hostile to reform — should be augmented and enriched with parties that, while striving for national unity and coherence, reflect and respect the distinct ideologies of a multiracial, multicultural society. To encourage full participation in the electoral process, elections should take place on weekends.

"Entrepreneurship." Free enterprise is a costly deception that leads to uninhibited capitalism. The wealth and resources of the country may be great for the rich but it's not so great for the average working stiff. If the economy is so solid, as economists have us believe, why were my Social Security "benefits" adjusted by a miserly percentage while food prices continue to soar, corporate giants add billions to their net worth — but pay no taxes — and six million workers depend on unemployment checks that are held hostage by wealthy politicians? Why is there plenty of money to keep a quarter of a million U.S. troops in 80 countries around the world, to finance the next Moon mission and give wings to the deranged obsession of colonizing Mars? Why do CEO's receive astronomical year-end bonuses, but most families cannot survive on one salary — that is if they still have a job?

An economy is "great" only when the lowest echelons of society can afford, without sacrifice, the basic necessities of life. My first initiative? Price controls on all basic commodities essential to the daily sustenance and wellbeing of the citizenry. Included in this roll-back: Rent, food, healthcare, pharmaceuticals, education, and public transportation. A loaf of bread, a stick of butter, a dozen eggs, a gallon of milk, and a head of lettuce would cost the same nationwide. I would tax luxury items that only the well-to-do can afford at 500 percent. I would also raise the minimum wage to reflect the artificially inflated and fraudulent cost of living so that a family of four can live in reasonable comfort and dignity on the salary of a single wage-earner, as was the case in 1956 when I immigrated to the U.S. Sure, hotels, lunch counters, restrooms, and public water fountains were segregated but if you were white, literate, and gainfully employed, life was a bowl of cherries. If you lost your job, you could find a better-paying one the very next day. A car cost about $2,000; a new house--$10,000. The average monthly rent was $88! Last, to restrain the largest fortunes from getting any larger, all income, including capital gains, dividends, and rents would be assessed at 90 percent. It's unjust when those who *own* have all the power and those who labor have none. Workers will have a say on how enterprises are run. Proceeds from wealth and inheritance taxes will be used to give a universal capital endowment of $150,000 to every citizen who turns 25.

The Second Amendment. I am conceptually opposed to this addendum, a misguided, hastily scripted, poorly worded, myopic codicil inserted in 1791, when the "Patriots" were fighting the British, and drafted to enable the formation and maintenance of a *"well-regulated militia"* but that in no way legalizes private ownership or arms-bearing privileges. What I object to most is how it has since been hijacked by the gun lobby and sanctified by gun fetishists. This love affair with guns is a uniquely American form of osmotic psychosis unrelated to the ill-conceived 18th century statute.

There were 690 mass shootings in the U.S. in 2023. These monstrosities are multiplying exponentially. Pro-gun lobbyists claim that the country suffers from a *"mental health problem,"* an odious lie echoed by the ultra-right to curry favor with their political base — all of them avid gun owners. The U.S has 342 million inhabitants ... and some 460 million firearms!

Gun-related violence has not prevented the vast majority of Americans from willfully misinterpreting this addon as they keep arming themselves to the teeth. At least 25 states allow (encourage) the purchase of firearms, including assault weapons, and several of these states allow (praise...) the open carrying of firearms. If there's a mental health problem in America, it's the inordinate love of guns and right-wing political deceit that looks the other way when innocent people are slaughtered. I often asked myself: What is it about their temperament that persuades Americans they are entitled to own guns? And then I remembered Hollywood and the small screen, which continue to bombard audiences with jaw-crushing slug fests and blood-spurting gun duels. I also remembered the revered he-man, the tough, silent bronc-bustin' pistol-packin' cigarillo-chompin' Bourbon-chuggin' enforcer who rides into the sunset and the desperado, a tragic figure who evokes inexplicable sympathy. I recalled Gunsmoke, The Virginian, Wagon Train, Rawhide, The Rifleman, Bonanza, High Noon, Have Gun: Will Travel, and Sudden Impact ("Make my day!"). And I harked back to generations of captive audiences reared to idolize—and emulate—vulgar thugs otherwise hyped as "folk heroes" (Daniel Boone, Davy Crocket, George Armstrong Custer, Buffalo Bill, Kit Carson, and Wyatt Earp), scumbags reminding us of America's "heroic" past and reanimating a nostalgia for that lawless epoch, the romance and legend of the Old West. One should not be surprised to learn that, upon visiting the U.S. in 1882, Irish poet and playwright, Oscar Wilde (1854-1900) famously wrote in a letter:

> *"Americans are certainly hero-worshipers, and always take their heroes from the criminal classes."*

Villain-worship and the Second Amendment have turned American men into high-strung, outwardly cocksure, inwardly skittish, overindulged, overfed, oversexed and sexually-conflicted, touchy and combative homophobes. Bursting with testosterone, they are desperately protective of their masculinity, enamored of their pickup trucks, and enraptured by their guns, which they keep lovingly oiled, loaded, and cocked.

Religion. Absolute separation between State and Church is vital to the health of a real democracy. Religion cannot be allowed to muscle in on the body politic. Religious institutions must survive on the charity of their parishioners. They should be stripped of their tax-exempt status and mandated to pay their fair share like everyone else. Nor should they be allowed to engage in commercial ventures. Any attempt by religious entities to influence court decisions, sway elections, manipulate education or dictate a faith-based code of conduct shall be vigorously resisted and penalized. The phrase, "under *god*," forced down America's throat by the ultra-Catholic lobby and added to the Pledge of Allegiance in 1954, shall be deleted. Freedom of religion is meaningless unless it includes freedom *from* religion.

The Supreme Court. The steadfast patron of the rich and powerful, the unelected enemy of democracy, the dinosaurian Supreme Court shall be tasked with adjudicating on the basis of law, not partisan politics or the justices' ideological leanings. Justices shall be elected, not appointed. They shall serve for a period not exceeding seven years, with a mandatory retirement age of 70.

States "rights." The doctrine leads to despotism and the tyranny of laws. States rights are shyster politics that regularly deny their citizens equal treatment under the law. They are at their ruthless worst in the most regressive and backward Southern, Great Plains, and Mountain states. The notion that states should enjoy special privileges by enacting their own laws, and that these laws can be transplanted in other states, is absurd. Says Dr. Ronald Feinman, Florida Atlantic University professor of American History, Government and Politics:

> *"Conservatives and Republicans have to promote states' rights, and for good cause. It allows states to deny their citizens the same rights, privileges, and benefits other states provide. Historically, it allowed states to have slaves; to promote segregation; to sanction capital punishment; to show no concern for the poor; to exploit labor through 'right-to-work' laws; to destroy the environment for industrial benefit; to victimize women and children; and to deny basic health care expansion under Medicaid and the*

Affordable Care Act."

States rights must be abridged and contained to harmonize with federal norms. No state can promulgate faith-based laws that restrict the rights of other states in matters of family planning. Thomas Jefferson's quest for a new form of self-government was based on the presumption that individual states — as if they were separate countries — have the right to enact their own laws. The so-called pursuit of "Life, Liberty, and Happiness," at best vague ideals, never itemized or clearly defined, enabled the enactment of "exceptionalist" provisos that allow states to independently *alter or abolish any form of governance deemed destructive,"* thus hastening the dismemberment of the *whole* to satisfy the claims of some of its constituent parts. *"A house divided against itself cannot stand."* America cannot for long endure the deep ideological chasm that sunders it. All signs point to secession and looming civil conflict.

Eminent domain. The claim that the government has the right to confiscate private land for public use is capricious, arbitrary, and routinely abused. It creates the foundation for mass evictions. "Fair compensation" is rarely fair. There have been few legislative attempts in the U.S. to control or define what is just compensation. When not deemed to be of crucial importance to national security, often an exaggerated pretext masking crass commercial interests, this self-granted practice should be subject to stringent exclusions. For example, a farm shall not be confiscated, nor a nature preserve commandeered to create a golf course, a raceway, a casino, or a resort. If eminent domain is left unchecked, virtually anything can be purloined and replaced with anything else.

Education. America's educational system needs to be revamped. The problem is that it is highly regulated — "finessed" is a more fitting term — at the state level. What Arkansas teaches about the Civil War (if anything remotely resembling the truth...) is eons away from what Massachusetts history books might reveal. Even public libraries are monitored by the states, sometimes even by individual counties. Books available at the New York Public Library might be banned (if not burned) in Georgia, Idaho, or Kansas. That's one.

Multiple-choice tests allow guessing, encourage test-wiseness, promote rote learning, offer no opportunity for students to express ideas, and provide no clues about their intellectual strengths and potential. Proficiency in history, geography, civics, and languages should be demonstrated in written essays and oral exams. Math problems should be solved manually (no calculators allowed) by showing sequentially, from premise to final tally, how that answer was reached. History books shall be purged of the lies and omissions that instill a false or misleading image of America's racist, imperialist, warmongering past. Teacher salaries shall be raised to give one of the most underrated professions the reverence it deserves. Public schools shall be enjoined from conducting prayer sessions, a devotional exercise that belongs in the home or house of worship, not in the classroom.

One should not be surprised that kids in the U.S. know close to nothing about the Holocaust. Most know even less about the methodical genocide of Native

Americans, slavery, the Civil War, the calculated annulment of rights painfully earned during Reconstruction, Jim Crow, segregation, and other shocking expressions of America's centuries-old disregard for equality and justice. Ironically, many teachers are just as ignorant on a large spectrum of topics. My teachers (in France) were highly educated, licensed to teach everything from algebra to zoology. It's not the case in the U.S. I shall not impugn the devotion or skill of some of the teachers I know but their illiteracy in certain subjects is staggering. The blame must also be shared with a new generation of students addicted to smartphones, selfies, social media, video games, and early, unprotected sex. Sixteen-to-19-year-olds spend an hour and twenty-five minutes per week reading compared to five hours and ten minutes per day on screens. In a study conducted among 1,500 young people aged seven to nineteen, interviewed from January 25 to February 2, 2024, we discover the extent of the problem. Diagnosis can be summed up in one word: screens. There was an Internet utopia, America let itself be dazzled. There is now an addictive lock-in with digital technology. We can speak of drugs, and in this respect, of a new opium war. At a time when we are inundated with permanent images, saturated with information—and misinformation—the screen is at our fingertips.

The dumbing down of America. America may be the richest, most powerful nation on earth, but it is one of the "free world's" most culturally blinkered and intellectually stifled. The coastal outer ring of urbane, sophisticated, progressive cities (Boston, New York, Philadelphia, Miami, Houston, Los Angeles, San Francisco, Portland,

and Seattle) does not represent the heartland, which remains hopelessly dogmatic, stubbornly conservative, and fanatically religious. Artistic, cultural, and educational institutions (theaters, museums, concert halls, opera houses, libraries, seats of higher learning) should benefit from generous government subsidies as they are essential in redressing America's climate of anti-intellectualism, pride of ignorance, and pervasive disdain of erudition.

Civil law. Couples wishing to tie the knot will have their heads examined, as will those planning to be fruitful and multiply on this obscenely overcrowded planet. Candidates for matrimony and parenthood will have to provide evidence that they are compatible as well as financially and emotionally fit to endure the rigors of wedlock and parenthood. Children do not ask to be born. Alimony, an extortionist device invented by shyster lawyers, shall be granted based on demonstrated need, not codified practice. The allowance granted the litigant shall not exceed what the penalized party can afford.

Healthcare. To reverse extreme concentrations of wealth and help usher a new era of participatory democratic socialism, federal taxes shall be raised on the very rich to subsidize a national health care system that protects *every* citizen, from the cradle to the grave, without the larcenous mediation of insurance companies. No paper-pusher in Washington must be allowed to tell physicians how to practice medicine.

Military adventurism. With the exception of *force majeure*, wars shall neither be declared nor prosecuted without the knowledge and assent of the electorate.

❦

The foregoing reforms are inspired by the nagging and long held conviction that the U.S. has turned into a mafia state. Its far-reaching tentacles must be amputated. My assessment of America is not one in which I take pleasure. Alas, as time passes, I find more evidence to support it. If America only shed its affectations and conceded that its concept of "liberty and justice for all" is a farce, that during its gestation and after its birth as a nation it engaged in brutal acts of banditry, first against indigenous populations — which it damn nearly liquidated — then against the forcibly imported Black labor it enslaved for more than two centuries; that it waged wars of imperialism and economic colonization; that its wealth is based on ruthless capitalism and the enrichment of privileged classes ... then I would say, O.K., the problem is not America, it's human nature. But when a nation goes to such lengths to proclaim its invincibility, to trumpet its fictional moral superiority, to vaunt its puritanism as it wallows in depravity, when it pompously grants itself the right to tell the rest of the world what to think and how to behave, when it meddles in other people's affairs in the name of "national security," (a slogan that must be understood to mean the safety of top-ranking government officials, wealthy elites, and financial institutions); when it ships the flower of its youth to die, be maimed or rendered mad in illegal, immoral, and unwinnable wars ... then it's not human nature anymore; it's a national mindset, a mentality, an attitude, a strange and troubling ingrained societal trait. A superpower that professes moral arguments to buttress its global vision for civil liberties and democracy cannot just abandon those standards in its senseless search for absolution. To those who claim that America "has changed," I argue that after a long and muted but troubled slumber disturbed by the election and reelection of the first Black president, America bared its fangs and revealed itself for what it always was: racist, xenophobic, jingoistic, greedy, violent, and boorish, at once prissy and promiscuous, parochial, and loudmouthed. The fictitious image that the U.S. has of itself, and which it peddles around the world, is a propagandist fib now debunked by the steady erosion of democracy, the rapid rise in fascism, and the combustible ideological rifts that threaten its existence. Of course, America will survive, transformed, hopelessly polarized, mutilated, grotesque, the disfigured remnant of a bold experiment gone wrong, the vestige of a quixotic dream Tomas Jefferson, John Adams, Ben, Franklin, Robert Sherman, and Robert Livingston, the framers of the Declaration of Independence, would not recognize and from which they would recoil in horror.

∽≫∾

The prognosis is poor. Hear me out. War is a profitable business but it's often the result of miscalculation rather than design. No one really wants war. No one is quite prepared to wage it, let alone win it. In time, words will get sharper, less guarded, and weapons, the antithesis of reason, will grow deadlier with each sound bite. No one will protest very loudly. Not a single voice will rise against the agitators who beat the drums of war. None will dare to send to hell the politicians who champion it, the economists who justify it, the bankers who finance it, the industries that thrive as it rages on, the generals who prosecute it—while the rest of us poor imbeciles are force-marched to the front to die or be maimed or driven mad in the name of some cockeyed patriotic grand dream, our intellect sedated, our vocal chords muted by fear, waning conviction, or apathy. A malignant tedium, a pervasive apathy, is subverting common sense.

Once random and episodic, famine is now spreading like wildfire across the globe as infant mortality skyrockets. There are other casualties. What little food can be scraped to keep the heart pumping is less than enough to nourish the mind. Two billion people are at risk of suffering irreversible brain damage. Soon, insane asylums will be full. More will be needed to contain a swelling tide of mental illnesses, but none will be built, and the overflow will spill into the streets, along with the homeless, the sick, the dead, and the dying. Everyone is armed. In cities, the haves wrangle with the have-nots. Looting, assaults, and other acts of violence soar during the long, ever-hotter summers as thousands die at the hands of vigilantes, mercenaries, morality brigades, and roaming bands of thugs. Justice is blind to injustice. Anti-war activists clash with flag-waving churls too old to be conscripted. Basic staples—bread, milk, eggs—are in short supply. Meat, when available at black-market prices, is rarely fresh. But hunger undermines common sense and everyone takes chances. If hunger and exposure kill the poor, it is often food poisoning that claims those who can still afford to eat. Water is now rationed. Some trickles in every other day. We may use it, Homeland Security has decreed, at our own risk. We may also breathe, if so compelled. The agency had the uncommon courtesy of refraining from issuing idiotic directives. The old panacea — crouch under a table and clasp your hands over your head, seal doors and windows with duct tape and plastic sheeting — is now the source of bitter jokes. Those who still believe in the power of prayer recite the Pater Noster and the 23rd Psalm. Others keep asking in every tongue known to man? *"Eli, Eli, lama sabakhthani?"* Lord, oh Lord, why has thou forsaken me?

These are not metaphors. Centuries pass and we keep on lecturing the simple-minded, punishing "heretics," pinning medals on the chests of professional killers while executing vulgar amateurs, enacting unenforceable laws, preaching unworkable ethics. And when our leaders and masters decide a little war is overdue, we let them drag us into battle. We sprinkle holy water on instruments of death, bless the juggernauts, and pray for victory because, after all, *god* must surely be on our side. We kill. We plunder. We die and others take our place: the young, the hope of all our tomorrows. There's the depravity, the reeking immorality of it all. Those who do not let it be forgotten are those who endured, are still alive, and can still reminisce and talk about it. Once they die, the memory of their agony will be erased forever. People have no interest in the past.

Since time immemorial, there have been idealists, young and old, who raised their voices against man's greed, corruptibility, decadence, and inhumanity. History 101. Nothing changed. The Jew named Jesus was crucified, not for flouting Judaism's codes but for wanting to enforce them. Carthusian monks have been silently, fervently praying day and night for peace since a disgruntled priest named Bruno and twelve followers fed up with the venal ways of the Church retreated to the monastery they built in the French Alps in 1084. Their prayers remain unheard and unheeded to this day. Galileo was tried by the Inquisition and died under house arrest for insisting that the Earth is round and that it revolves around the Sun, not the other way around. Countless dreamers have been martyred on every continent for preaching love, equality, and justice, or for telling inconvenient truths. Wasn't I targeted for assassination some thirty years ago and didn't I have to abscond in the middle of the night when I identified the killers of a young Mayan tribal counselor (he was shot, stabbed, and scalped) who advocated for the return of ancestral lands stolen by white settlers? Weren't millions of Native Americans massacred so that intruders could spread out over their domains and enjoy *"life, liberty, and the pursuit of happiness"*? Weren't Gandhi and Martin Luther King slain for preaching non-violence? What about 250 years of slavery and another few decades of Jim Crow in an America that, to this day, has the audacity to proclaim itself righteous and a model for the world? Weren't Lincoln, JFK and RFK killed for their "progressive" views? Wasn't Nelson Mandela imprisoned for 27 years on a rat-infested island for defying South Africa's heinous apartheid? Aren't Russian dissidents targeted for death (and dying) as we speak? And aren't innumerable Palestinians humiliated, persecuted, and liquidated by an increasingly totalitarian and ultra-religious Israel that seems to have forgotten recent history?

The "revolution" I have been advocating calls for a moral and intellectual transformation of man, not a blood-soaked upheaval. But that too is a quixotic, unachievable goal. Man does not and will not change. The little planet that we continue to plunder and rape will do just fine after the last Cain slays the last Abel. We are not *god*'s "masterpiece." We are a freak of evolution and nature will sooner or later exact its rightful revenge upon the flawed creatures who defy it. The sooner the better because what we face ahead will be unendurable. Is it any wonder that some of us die insane? Madness is often the refuge of last resort for those who can no longer cope with reality. Of course it's totally out of our control, irrevocable, universal. Short-term, life on Earth will become unlivable. Long-term, as the Sun's life cycle comes to an end, Earth itself will cease to be. A "better" world is the stuff of fantasy. Entropy does not play dice with the universe. Everything moves from a state of order to a state of disorder, from stability to chaos. The process is irreversible. Meanwhile, like ants, we will spend our lives hoarding and digging in. A calamitous future looms ahead. Don't say I didn't warn you. And don't pretend you didn't know. Surely, if it happened tomorrow, it'll happen yesterday.

TRIBUTES
Why I write

This book was conceived long before I set out to construct it piece by piece from a patchwork of childhood reminiscences, random musings hastily recorded on a pad in the dead of night, and simmering emotions spiced up by the steady pace of history endlessly retold, relived, betrayed. Several life-altering events and a harvest of images and insights gleaned during my years as an itinerant journalist also contributed to its protracted and painful gestation.

I must confess that when I decided to give this project wings, I was seduced by the notion that I would be penning the book I always wanted to read—an irreverent, vexing polemic, part exposé, part history, part satire, part plausible conjecture—a tract that could somehow help galvanize a world mired in myth and sanctified deception. Fighting windmills, as the Man of la Mancha noted after two, maybe three valiant but impossible quests, is pointless. The giants of blind faith, conformity, and entrenched traditions are formidable foes, and common sense is swiftly submerged in the quicksand of ideological rigidity and fanaticism.

Whatever idealism I might have mistakenly thought I possessed in my youth has long since been replaced by cynicism and disgust at man's inability or unwillingness to advance far from his primal state. Assumptions, like doctrinal beliefs, have an academic appeal—it is interesting to plumb the limits of human imagination—

but they do not hold for me the same allure as the observable, palpable universe around me. This may explain why I stopped reading novels some 30 years ago. I find non-fiction — in all its incarnations — infinitely more illuminating.

As I reviewed the manuscript one last time in search of stray typos and skewed syntax, I was reminded, as the French saying concludes, *"Tout passe, tout casse, tout lasse."* [Everything wanes, everything breaks down, everything becomes tiresome.] Everything includes anything that time renders irrelevant, including the unexceptional but candid work you were brave enough to peruse. I had no illusions about its utility or merit. I was often tempted to give up. I just kept going. It is a habit of mine, perhaps inherited, later instilled in journalism school, then honed during a long and bumpy journalistic career, to tell inconvenient truths. This "addiction" is not without risk: Lost jobs, the hostility of readers, the alienation of friends and family members, and two death threats, one so serious and imminent that I had to abscond in the middle of the night. I'm 86; I haven't given up. In the process, I learned two things: One, when you keep silent in the face of injustice, you become in a way complicit; two, when you bury your head in the sand, you risk getting run over.

The book I always wanted to read, the one that impeaches Homo sapiens and fearlessly exposes his wickedness and immeasurable idiocy, I felt, had not yet been written, not by Habakkuk or Ezekiel in their apocalyptic Old Testament warnings, nor by John's demented rants in the New; not in the allegorical torments tallied in Dante's *Divine Comedy*; not in Aldous

Huxley's *Ape and Essence*, which envisions a post-nuclear nightmare; nor in Ray Bradbury's chilling *There will Come Soft Rain*, which surveys humanity's self-immolation. Nothing had been rendered, I feared, not by the written word (or Hieronymus Bosch's terrifying painted evocations of divine retribution) which remotely approximated the rancor and grief I bear as I surveyed mankind's ossified ignorance, vulgarity, and malevolence —least of all in my own feeble indictment.*

I had no choice.

❧

I am indebted first and foremost to my parents, learned, urbane, open-minded, for instilling a love of books, music, art, philosophy, and science, for sparing me the enslavement of religious indoctrination—which, I am convinced, irreparably mutilates many children emotionally—and for enduring, if not always endorsing, my wildest escapades. To my mother, a selfless, unassuming, cultured woman of great refinement who insisted that human nature corrupts humans, I owe my reverence for beauty and symmetry, and my love of animals. From my father, a caring, iron-willed, and incorruptible country doctor who abhorred ostentation, pretense, and all manner of affectation, I learned that self-esteem and respect for truth confer infinitely greater gifts than money, material comfort, or celebrity.

I salute my teachers, those I pleased when I applied myself and those I exasperated. Their erudition,

---

* *One Last Dream*, by W. E. Gutman, © 2012, CCB Publishing.

pedagogical skills, and saintly patience for the lazy, unfocused, mercurial, and rebellious student I was, helped lay the foundations on which I would erect a lifetime career of endless beginnings.

I can never sufficiently acknowledge the immense influence several writers, poets, and philosophers have had on the constantly evolving person I would become and, by extension, on the ideas I would champion. Their prose, verses, insights, and eye-opening reflections resonate as intensely today as they did in the days of my youth. Most were French. One was denied a Christian funeral for penning vitriolic anti-clerical tracts. Four were imprisoned, the first for denouncing the bestiality of colonialism; the second—the son of a prostitute—for vagabondage, lewd acts, and other offenses against public decency; the third for stretching the limits of literary freedom in pamphlets that mixed raw eroticism with civil disobedience. The fourth spoke for the common man and rose with uncommon bravery against the profligacy of the clergy and the decadence of the military establishment.

Three were Russian. One of them, a novelist, essayist, and journalist, explored human psychology in the social, political, and spiritual milieu of his time. His works are populated with neurotics and lunatics, the kind who become pope, king, dictator, tyrant, president. It took as deranged a genius like him to understand and paint the frailties, aberrations, and horrors of life. Reading him is like descending into a snake pit of insanity. The poor man had epilepsy. He was sentenced to death for writing anti-tsarist articles (the sentence was commuted at the last moment). He spent four years in a Siberian prison camp, followed by six years of compulsory military service in exile—enough to madden anyone. The second, a ruthless satirist, imparts surrealism and the grotesque with an unusual aura of normality. The third, the one that shocked me to my core, was a professional revolutionary, and theorist of anarchism. The man, an odious antisemite, was a closet authoritarian who condoned violence. I did agree with him when he remarked,

> *"Everything will pass, and the world will perish but [Beethoven's] Ninth Symphony will endure forever."*

My other mentors wrote in Arabic, English, Dutch, German, Sanskrit, and Spanish. Three hailed from Ireland. One did not survive the spurious puritanism of his Victorian milieu. The other died insane—as do those who seek shelter from the battering storm of reality in the sanctuary of delirium. The third was excommunicated for trying to resolve the conflict between religious dogma and secular knowledge, and for highlighting the depth of human ignorance. All were freethinkers, iconoclasts, rebels, defenders of secularism, all deceased, but whose heterodoxy and reformist ideas still inspire new generations of resisters, heroes, and martyrs.

It is with equal reverence that I thank my friends, few as they are, attentive and loyal, whose encouragement helped immensely as I battled illness, introspection, and self-criticism during the gestation of this and other works. I must also credit my detractors, far more numerous, for reinforcing my conviction that in this era of lies and unreason all opinions have some equivalence and negligible weight but that only the truth, scarce but all-seeing and easily distorted, unnerving and often cruel, must prevail. Sadly, the evanescent nature of history's impact on future generations does not include a built-in sense of anticipation for the horrors to come — nor an iota of scruple, revulsion or remorse for the horrors unfolding on our watch while we idle along in serene unconcern as hatred and imbecility triumph.

Born in Paris, W. E. Gutman is a veteran journalist, editor, columnist, and published author. A former press attaché, he reported from Central America from 1994 to 2006.

www.ingramcontent.com/pod-product-compliance
Lightning Source LLC
Chambersburg PA
CBHW021159010426
R18062100001B/R180621PG41931CBX00039B/71